# THE INVISIBLE YOU

## MARGARET RUTH

*"HE thinks in secret, and it comes to pass.*
*Environment is but his looking-glass."*
*James Allen*

Library of Congress Catalog Card No. 82-70544
ISBN 0-9608130-0-4

Published by: The Broome Closet
12433 Cumpston Street
North Hollywood, CA 91607

# INTRODUCTION

Neville was my teacher*. From him I learned to believe in my *self*. Neville knew the truth which sets all men free and he shared it with all who would listen. He used to say, "If truth could ever be told so that it could be understood, it would be believed." This is what I have attempted to do, for I have found my own wonderful human imagination to be Him of whom Moses and the prophets spoke, Jesus of Nazareth. In the following pages I have tried to introduce Him to you. He is not near, for nearness implies separation. He is not a vapor flowing through, around and about you, but the very core of your being. He is your awareness, your consciousness. He is your power-filled imagination!

Each chapter in this little book is composed of a thought based upon the truth that you are God incarnate. No chapter depends upon the other for interpretation, but in each thought I have tried to make the truth as simple as possible. I have shared my own visions and experiences with you, as well as those of my friends. This I have done in the hope that they will encourage you to believe in *self*, for buried in you is the only true God, whose name is I AM.

Put these truths into practice and you will gain the mastery of your life, for my words are true. They have the power to change your life if you will but open the door of your mind and let them in.

---

*His lectures form the basis of each chapter.

*To my husband, Ray, for loving me and allowing me the time and space to grow.*

# TABLE OF CONTENTS

## THE INVISIBLE YOU

### "God is Spirit" (John 4:24)

God is your invisible thought. It is he who creates your visible world. Invisible thoughts create visible acts for God, the invisible you, is the only creator of and actor in the world. Let me illustrate my point by telling you about our cat. Tiger has been around our house for many years. He is an outdoor cat who spends the greater part of his day "guarding" our house from his vantage point on the sunny front porch. One day, as I backed the car out of the garage, I felt the left rear tire run over something, heard a scream and saw a dark form disappear around the house. Tiger was nowhere to be seen and I realized what I had done. Frantic, I called a friend who drove me to the veterinary hospital where Tiger was given a shot and left to rest. Returning home my friend said, "I knew someone would run over Tiger because he is always lying in the driveway. I have been expecting this for sometime."

An invisible thought was planted in the mind of my friend and, since there is only one mind, the invisible me made his thought visible. This is how God creates. The thoughts of my friend were secret, yet they set the stage for the unseen "I" to fulfill, for God (I am) is the cause and the consequence of everything in the world.

Though invisible, you are forever imagining, forever acting. While wearing your garment of sense you may not see immediate changes in your world, but changes will come for God cannot fail. Perhaps your friend is ill and, though unseen, you are imagining him well, but he dies to your eyes. Have you failed? No, for there are worlds within worlds within worlds and you are creating in every one of them. Imagine and *let* it be true! God made you in his image and then became your invisible imagination thereby making you a living soul. Use this creative power within you and your living soul will become a life-giving spirit.

While lunching one day at a restaurant near her home, a friend saw some lovely rose-colored water glasses on the table and asked to buy them. The proprietor told her that was impossible as the glasses were manufactured in the east and the supply was limited. Returning home, my friend imagined eight water glasses, rose in color, sitting on her dining room table. Every day she drank from those glasses and enjoyed their beauty. One month later she returned to the restaurant where she was introduced to the new owner. Telling him of her love and desire for the glasses, he excused himself and returned with a gift . . . a box of not eight but sixteen lovely rose-colored glasses!

If you know what you want, invisibly claim it. Do not be concerned as to what people will say, whether they will think it right or wrong, simply ignore the evidence of your senses and claim you have what you want. Start now to live a full, wonderful life, for you are all imagination and only imagination creates.

Want more money? Then open the western gate called "touch" and touch your imaginary paycheck.

Want to travel? Let the invisible you view the world from abroad. Imagine the person you want to be and walk in that consciousness. Live in your imagination and everything, seemingly detached and independent of you, will join together and your desire will become real.

"When weary man enters his cave he meets his Savior in the grave. Some find a female garment there and some a male, woven with care." (Wm. Blake) Man is God and God is your invisible reality. It is he who wears a male or female garment. You have been crucified with Christ, nevertheless you live, yet not you but Christ who lives in you. The life you now live in the flesh you live by faith in the Son of God who loved you and gave himself for you.

Everything is woven within you by the invisible you called God. You act and the world responds. The clothes you wear and the chair you now sit in were first imagined, then brought into being. Invisibly appropriate health, wealth and success, for your life depends upon the activity of the invisible you. Become aware of your invisibility and join the divine society by becoming one of the gods who creates.

Every moment of time God begets him*self* in you and God cannot fail. Think the best of your*self* and others, for you are thought and, though invisible, you are God,

**"Examine your*self* to see if you are holding to the faith. Test your*self*. Do you not realize that Jesus Christ is in you?" (11 Cor 13:5)**

I s it possible to examine your*self* and find Jesus Christ? Yes, when you know He is your human imagination! This is how it is done. If health is your desire, imagine you are healthy. Then, as the days pass by, examine your thoughts and see if you are remaining faithful to that state. If you are, your thoughts will flow from that idea. Hold to your faith by controlling your thoughts and when health is yours you will have found Jesus Christ, for He is the cause of all life. If harmony or wealth is your desire, test your*self* by viewing your world. Is it peopled with harmony and wealth? I hope so, for your world always reveals your belief in *self*.

Let me tell you about a friend of mine. Her 16 year old daughter had run away from home. Very upset and longing to have her back, my friend called the police, chased down every lead and hired a private detective, but the girl was not to be found. Finally, in desperation, my friend went to bed and created this mental act. She imagined hearing the key in the front door, watching the knob turn and seeing her daughter standing in the doorway. Night after night she repeated her imaginal act, falling asleep consciously talking to her loving daughter. A week later the girl returned home and they are now together again expressing a mutual love and understanding which had never been possible before. My friend had the courage to examine her*self* and the belief that if she controlled her imagination her world would reshape itself to reflect her new thoughts, and it did.

The Bible tells the story of the awakening of your soul, for God had to fall asleep in order to dream your life into being. You may not realize it, but the power that sustains the universe is in you, for you are the invisible power and wisdom of God, called Christ. Use this power, the power of consciousness, and consciously assemble a mental act. Then your mind will activate that which the assemblage implies and you will experience its effect in your world. All things, good and evil, are waiting to come into your life, but they cannot come unless their assemblage is created. My friend assembled a mental image and her mind activated that which the assemblage implied.

Intensity always foreshortens the time of fulfillment. Build a fire under your desire and, just like heating water, the results will depend upon the adjustment of the flame. Your water can take five minutes or five hours to boil. And so it is with your power. Its degree of intensity is up to you.

There is no outside God. He is in you, individualized *as* you. The word "person" means "the mask of the actor." Your garment of flesh is God's mask, for he is weaving you out of imagination. His power had to reach the limit of contraction in order to become you. Start now to consciously use your imagination. Interfere with the purely mechanical structure of your brain and you will begin to affect life rather than reflect it.

Imagination fulfills itself in what your life becomes. Believe in chance and you are enslaved by your belief. Become a free man and walk knowing your imagination is fulfilling it*self.* Persist and you will move from the slavery of thought to its freedom. Imagine for the sheer joy of creating. Assemble your imagery and as you sustain it everyone needed to fulfill your drama will appear and play his part. Do not be concerned with what others are thinking; simply persist in believing you have what you want and you will receive it.

Nothing is impossible to God. There is no such thing as competition. If you can conceive a thought you can possess it. Can you imagine God saying, "If this doesn't work I will try something else?" Awake to your true creative power and you will see cooperation, not competition.

Go down to the potter's house (your mind) and listen to your thoughts on their wheel. If those of your friend are not pleasant, he is spoiled. But do not throw him away, instead change your thoughts of him as it seems good to you, the potter, to do. Then watch, and you will see your friend has been reworked into another vessel, just as you had imagined.

You can be as successful or noble as you want to be if you will but think successful, noble thoughts. But take care as to how you build upon your imagination for no other foundation can anyone lay than that which is laid, which is Jesus Christ. Build with gold, silver, precious stones, wood, hay or stubble, but remember, your work will become manifest for the day will reveal it. If your work survives you will receive a reward, but if it is burned you will suffer loss, though you will be saved, but only as through fire. Feel fear and you will suffer loss for you are building a world of fear. Persist and that which you are afraid of will be yours.

Let no one tell you what you should have, for the world is yours and all within it. Simply assemble the imagery necessary to fulfill your desire. Live in that knowledge and your desire will come about so naturally you will be tempted to believe it would have happened anyway. But always remember, nothing happens by chance. Only by an activity of your imagination (known or unknown) can it be brought into being. Always imagining, it is easy to forget your thoughts of the day, but you cannot harvest what you do not plant and all thoughts are planted by your imagination.

God, he who is always imagining, creating and recreating, loved you so much he wove himself into your brain. Though you seem to have a beginning, you are the Lord of Lords, the alpha and omega, the beginning and the end. Believe in your*self* and you will believe your*self* into being!

## AN IMMACULATE CONCEPTION

**"This is he who came by water and blood,
Jesus Christ, not by water only but by
water and blood." (1 John 5:6)**

E very thought is an immaculate conception, and when incarnated it is given human parentage. A virgin thought flows into the mind in the form of a desire. Give that desire solidity through feeling and the blood has been added making the birth of your desire assured.

Have you ever thought of living elsewhere? Perhaps a new house or apartment? If you have, your new house was created the moment you had the thought, for every thought is a breath of life. But thoughts can be aborted through doubt and limitation, and when this happens your water (your desire) has gone to waste. But you can add the blood by moving into your house. Then you have breathed the breath of life into your desire and its birth is guaranteed. This is how it is done. Stand in the center of your imaginary living room and mentally walk across the floor. Touch the furniture. See the objects on the wall and the view from the window. Turn on the stereo and enjoy its music as you sip a glass of wine. Feel the thrill of possession and you are mixing water and blood; thereby pulling life out of death. Then wait, for the day will come when you will give birth to that which was formerly only a thought.

A desire, by it*self*, can produce nothing. Only as your desire is mixed with feeling (the blood of reality) can its birth occur. And, just as water and blood are the symbols of every natural birth, so it is in the spirit world. Desire must be mixed with action (the feeling of fulfillment) in order for birth to occur.

Jesus, your all-inclusive savior, will give you anything you ask for in his name. Claim you are secure by feeling secure and you have asked in his name. Feel happy, healthy and content and He has saved you from sadness, illness and discontentment. Feel love and you have made love alive, for your world is held together by the glue of consciousness. Remember, although everything seems to be outside of you, "What is seen is made out of things which do not appear." (Heb 11:3) Your world never has been and never will be any other place than in your own mind, your own wonderful human imagination.

"God is spirit and he who worships him does so in spirit and in truth." (John 4:24) Spirit is not a church, a synagogue, a statue on the wall or anything you can turn to on the outside. Your mind is the spiritual temple of the living God and water and blood are its functions. Jesus poured water into a stone jar and wine was released. (John 2) Your world is as solid and real as stone while your desire as fluid as water. Give your desire the sense of stone by feeling its presence and form, and you will drink the wine of fulfillment.

Several years ago I met Mary, a delightful poet. Her poetry I did not understand, but her desire to express herself, I did. At the time she did not have a typewriter, so I loaned her mine. One day I called her apartment only to discover that she (and my typewriter) had moved, leaving no forwarding address. Friends did not know her whereabouts and I was at a loss as to what to do, so I turned to Jesus, my all-inclusive savior, and asked for my typewriter "in his name." This is what I did. Seating my*self* in my favorite chair in the living room I began to think about my typewriter; its size, shape, color and weight. Then I placed it on my dining room table, removed its cover and inserted some paper. Feeling the keys beneath the tips of my fingers, I gave the typewriter the sense of stone as I typed out a thank you note to my friend, thanking her for its return. Then I relaxed into a momentary sleep.

As the weeks passed by, I persisted in seeing the typewriter on the table and then one day a friend called. She had been looking over some old Christmas cards and had found the address of Mary's parents. That day I wrote Mary a letter. One month later I returned from shopping to find my typewriter sitting on my dining room table, just as I had imagined. Mary had left it with my husband and gone on her way. I have never seen Mary again, but I knew what I had done. I gave my desire, my immaculate conception, the solidity of stone by feeling its presence. Then I drank the wine of fulfillment and its birth appeared in my world. I moved from the state of loss to the state of fulfillment, and you can too.

Now, a state of consciousness is a non-existing nothingness. It is your invisible *self*-begotten child. Unaided by another, your present state was conceived and carried in your mind. As an immaculate conception, you gave it virgin birth. Detach your*self* from your present state and enter another through feeling. Persist, and the evidence of your present state will vanish from your sight. Awaken Christ, your creative power, and move from a passive into an active state of mind.

Instead of passively surrendering to appearances, actively make everything subject to your imagination. Assume the feeling of your wish fulfilled and you will become the active ruler of your world. In the state of Adam you are asleep and passive. But let Christ awaken in you and your active mind will affect life and no longer reflect it.

Know what you want. Look into the face of your savior by seeing your desire clearly in your mind's eye. Use your imagination consciously and your mind will expand to higher and higher levels of awareness. Jacob saw God standing on the top of his consciousness ladder. You may think you are on the lowest rung, but you are destined to reach the top and know your*self* to be the one God who was before that the world was. Conscious of being, you died in order to be conscious of being you. Your death was complete forgetfulness. It is now time to awaken and remember.

> "Man should not stay a man
> His aim should higher be.
> For God will only gods
> Accept as company."     . . . Unknown

Your mortal body, though dead, is made alive by your imagination. Activate your mind by giving your immaculate conception the right of birth and you will discover that something comes out of nothing. That life comes out of death, for imagination *always* creates reality.

## THE ART OF DYING

**"I die daily" (1 Co 15:31)**

B egin now to learn the art of dying, for only as you die can you live. Die to poverty by living in wealth. Sickness will die when health is made alive. How is it done? By consciousness. The consciousness of God—that power which created and sustains the universe—is your consciousness with its power decreased. If you will but increase the intensity of your imagination (your consciousness), greater and greater worlds will be yours.

Have you ever read the story of Moses as recorded in the 34th chapter of the Book of Deuteronomy? It tells of his journey from the plains of Moab to the promised land of Jericho. It is said that Moses was not allowed to enter the promised land and "Though his eye was not dim or his natural force abated, Moses died and no one knows his burial place to this day." (De 34:1-7)

The Bible is filled with stories of the mind, and every character recorded there is within you. As Moses, you have the power to draw any state of consciousness out of your*self.* Leave the state of lack by closing the door of your mind on thoughts of limitation. Then open the door of plenty by contemplating the feeling of its possession. See, touch, taste, smell and feel the joy of fulfillment. Then give your new state the breath of life by filling your body with joy and let its exhalation explode throughout every pore. Your creative power, as Moses, is now dead and no one knows where it is buried. But you do, for having drawn your desire out of *self*, your creation is made alive. Become conscious of a state's existence, and your creative power is buried in it. Think from the state and your power makes it live. Then desire, as Moses, dies, for you cannot desire that which you already have. But, although Moses dies, his eye is not dim or his natural force abated. If doubt should creep in, regain the consciousness of your desire. Die to denial, regardless of its physical reality, by persisting in living conscious of your desire, and it will become your only reality. Remember, Moses (your creative power) is buried in you and will rise in you whenever you call him forth.

God crucified him*self* on you that you might live. Imitate him by crucifying your*self* on your desire. Belief is God's nails. Make your desire alive by nailing your*self* to and believing in its reality. Crucify your*self* to the feeling of fulfillment, for crucifixion always precedes resurrection. Death always comes before life. Crucify your*self* to your dream. Completely abandon *self* and, as you live in the consciousness of your desire, it will become your reality.

A state dies by detachment. Detach your*self* from the state of confusion, and harmony will be yours. Die every day, for every death is a lifting of the divine image. Die to ill health, poverty or conflict by feeling health, wealth or harmony. States are permanent and, like cities, remain forever for anyone to enter or depart from. A state, just like a city, does not care whether you enter it or not, nor is it concerned with how long you stay. Your entrance into a state, as well as your departure from it, is completely up to you.

Jesus told his disciples to go to the crossroads where two ways meet. There they would find a colt on which no man had ever sat. Your emotion, symbolized as a colt, may be difficult to mount. But you must ride your colt (emotion) into the land of fulfillment (called Jerusalem) without being thrown by reason. Go to the crossroads where what you are and what you want to be meet. Untie your beast and catch the feeling of the joy of possession. Ride this feeling into Jerusalem by completely abandoning your*self* to your dream. Die to your old way of thinking and live in the new, for all life is yours. You are now tied to that which you are conscious of. If you do not love it, bear your cross and cross over into heaven by being conscious of that which you do love.

Everything in life is interrelated. Solutions always come out of conflicts. Your present state seemed like heaven when you first entered it. But heaven can become hell as conflicts arise. Therefore, die to conflict by moving into a new state. Then, if you discover that it is not as heavenly as you thought it would be, move on into another. This is how you grow and outgrow as you travel the road to an awakened imagination.

Keyed low, your imagination will intensify as you lift it up. Demand things to change by knowing what you want and yielding to their consciousness. Clothe a state in flesh by consciously moving into it, for everything remains only a state until it is yielded to. Even your past can be given new birth if you so desire. A lady I know poured boiling water on her hand and unburned it. Lying on the bed, in great pain, she imagined filling the teapot with boiling water and pouring tea into her cup. This she did over and over again until she fell asleep drinking her tea. When she awakened, several hours later, there was no pain or trace of a burn.

My friend unmade her past and you can too. A terrible mistake can be revised and changed if you are willing to die, and there is nothing in life like death. Die to lack by living in fulfillment. Practice the art of dying and you will discover that death is the best thing in life.

## THE CANDLE OF THE LORD

**"The Spirit of man is the candle of the Lord. Job remembered and walked through darkness by the light of the candle on his head." (Job 29:3)**

In the Book of Luke it is said that when Jesus was full of the Holy Spirit he found him*self* in the wilderness. This is true, for when you see the world as subjectively related to you, your bewildered state becomes a wilderness. But, as an inner and deeper understanding is yours, you are mystically baptized and the candle on your head is lit. Then all of the dark caverns of the brain grow luminous and you walk through darkness by the light of imagination.

Every being in the world is subjectively related to you. You have the power to give them beauty for ashes, joy for mourning and the garment of praise for the spirit of heaviness. And when you do, you become a tree of righteousness, the planting of the Lord to the glory of God.

A gentleman I know dreamed of being rich. His prayer was to become a millionaire. He came to see me on borrowed money and we began to imagine together. Closing my eyes to the obvious I heard him say, "Now I am a Texas millionaire." I congratulated him and shared the good news with my husband. Then I felt the thrill which comes from the fulfillment of desire, opened my eyes and we talked of other things.

Returning to Texas, the bus stopped in Phoenix where the gentleman decided to call a friend, an artist he admired very much but had not seen for many years. Learning that the man had terminal cancer and had been praying for help, the gentleman remained in Phoenix to care for his friend. While there he was given the responsibility of disposing of paintings valued at over two million dollars of which he received a 60% commission. All of this took place in less than one month's time.

This is how you give beauty for ashes, joy for mourning and open the prison doors to those who are financially, socially, intellectually, or physically bound. You can do it too, for everyone in the world has the power to light that candle. Jesus was sent to preach glad tidings to the meek, and you are meek when your mind is so disciplined you can set it to any task and have it faithfully executed. Glad tidings will be yours when you use your power of possession, for you cannot desire that which you already possess.

The responsibility of a disciplined mind is to set every captive free. This is done by revision. If you know someone who is financially imprisoned, bring him before your mind's eye and see him embody a wealthy state. Persist, and your thoughts will give reality to his world. When your mind is thus awakened, you will no longer react and surrender to appearances. You will act and create a life of your own choosing.

Begin now to light your candle by reliving the scenes of your day. If something unpleasant happened, rewrite the script. Relive the revised scene by giving it all of the tones of reality. Fall asleep revising your day and you will awaken to a transformed tomorrow, for your thoughts never recede into the past, but are forever advancing into the future to confront you.

A dear friend of mine, always in a hurry, slipped on the second step of her concrete stairway and fell to the sidewalk some twenty steps below. Feeling dizzy and ill, neighbors helped her back into the apartment. Lying on the bed, she closed her eyes and forced her mind to do her will. Retracing her steps, she moved from the kitchen to the front door. Descending the stairs she felt her foot slip on the second step. Then she stopped the action and returned to her apartment. This scene was repeated over and over again until my friend was able to descend the stairs in a normal, natural manner. Then she fell asleep shopping for groceries.

Awakening several hours later, my friend went into the kitchen to bake a pie, only to discover that she did not have the necessary ingredients. Remembering they had been purchased in a dream, she wondered if the fall had also only been a dream, for my friend had revised her day so well there was not even a bruise to share its memory.

Nothing is impossible when you exercise and awaken your power called Christ. Revise your day. Feel its reality. Sleep in that consciousness and you will discover that pure imagination will harden into objective reality. Light your candle by the conscious use of your imagination. See the world as subjectively real and no longer objectively so and you will walk through darkness by the light of Christ. The historicity of the Bible supported and comforted you in the past, but when you are baptized in the river Jordan your mind is washed of all literal concepts. Exposed to the psychological meaning of scripture only, you are bewildered, but not robbed of Jesus. Instead, as an inner and deeper understanding returns, you find he is your only reality.

In the Book of Mark we are told, "Whatever you ask in prayer believe you have received it and you will. But when you stand praying, forgive if you·have anything against anyone that your Father might forgive you your trespasses. But if you do not forgive, neither will your Father forgive you." (Mk 11:24-26) (Notice, there is no limitation placed on your request. All you are required to do is believe you have received it.) But this very statement is followed by the requirement that you must forgive. These seem to be two different thoughts, but they are truly one, for the only way you can forgive anyone is by consciousness. Forgive a friend who is ill by being conscious of his good health. Do that and your prayer for health will be answered. I forgave the poor man by praying (being conscious of) his wealth. My act of forgiveness changed my consciousness and by that act my heavenly Father forgave me.

Light your candle by determining your desire and then appropriate it. You can have anything you want, for the world is yours and all within it. Find Christ and you have found the light of the world. He is the spirit of God, the candle of the Lord, individualized as your own wonderful human imagination. You are Jesus, now, for your power and wisdom, called Christ, has revealed you as the Lord.

Give up all belief in powers outside of *self*, for you are the living bread which came down from heaven. Believe in *self* and, as you experience scripture, you partake of the body of Jesus Christ. Rooted in the Lord, you came into the world as his son. Eat the bread of eternal life and you will leave the world as the Father knowing, "I and my Father are one." (Joh 10:30)

But while you are here, use the law of identical harvest by assuming you have what you want. Believe your seemingly false assumptions are true, and your desires will become facts. Use your power to create, for every objective fact in the world is projected from this invisible you. As the light and power of the world, you light an invisible state with consciousness, and your power projects its shadow in the world of time and space.

Remember, life is an activity of imagination. Imagine a state and it is made alive. As God's son you give life to every state you are conscious of. Awaken to your invisibility by claiming you are God the Father, the life-giving Spirit of the world.

**"I am the living bread which came down from heaven."**
**(Joh 6:51)**

"Jesus Christ, who was in the form of God, emptied him*self* and took on the form of a slave, born in the likeness of men. Being found in human form he humbled him*self* and became obedient unto death, even death upon a cross." (Phil 2:6,8) You are that man, for you are Jesus Christ. Wearing the consciousness of God you emptied your*self* of that awareness and took on the form of a slave, born in the likeness of men. Being found in human form you entered the state of amnesia. Now playing the part of Saul, the demented king, you have forgotten who you are. But one day your memory will return and, as you play the part of Paul, your kingdom will be restored and you will be crowned the king of kings and lord of Lords forever.

Many years ago I felt my*self* to be spirit, infinite light and air. I seemed to have no circumference, no body, no limitation. I simply was. Looking down, through infinite space, I saw what appeared to be an ant, as its body was so small. Desiring to know it better I created an elongated wooden box. Then darkness overwhelmed me and restriction became so great I felt as though I could not breathe. Holes appeared for eyes and I found my*self* in a body with arms and hands, legs and feet. It could not operate it*self*, but moved only at my command. Then darkness and restriction overcame me and I slept.

How long I remained asleep I do not know, but suddenly, in a burst of freedom, I broke the bonds of limitation and felt my*self* once more one with the universe. Light as air, free as the wind and shining like the sun I looked down to see what appeared to be my mortal body lying on a bed. Friends and relatives were staring at it in silent meditation. As I entered the room I heard my husband say, "She's dead." Looking at the body in shocked amazement, I shook my husband and cried, "Here I am. I am not dead, but alive! That body cannot die for it was never alive. I was its life. Turn around and you will see, though it was mine, it is not me."

This was a true vision, for every child born of woman could not breathe unless spirit, infinite light and air, encased itself within that form to be born in the likeness of men. Being found in human form and no longer aware of being spirit, God's son bears his cross (your body) and dreams your world into being. But when your journey is over you will awaken to your true identity. The limitation of a human form will cease to be, and you will once more know you are the life giving spirit of the world. Conscious of being one, you entered a world of many. Turn around and awaken to your true identity, for you are the one Lord, one Spirit, one God and Father of all.

Starting your journey in the state of Adam, it will be finished in the state of Jesus Christ, for a plan of salvation, described in scripture as God's autobiography, has been prepared for your return. While wearing the cross of man you will experience every eternal state of consciousness personified in scripture. Then David will call you Father and God's autobiography will be yours.

## FORGIVENESS OF SIN

**"If you forgive the sins of another they are forgiven, but if you retain the sins of any they are retained."**
**(Joh 20:23)**

Y ou have the power to forgive your sins and those of another, and if you do it they are forgiven. But if you retain any sin, it is retained. How is this done? By imagination!

If you know someone who is poor and would like to be rich, ill and desires health, unhappy and wants to be happy, forgive him by thinking he is rich, healthy and happy. Forgive your*self* in the same manner. Knowing what you want, claim its possession. Become conscious of it and you will sin no more. But if you return to your old pattern of thinking (about your*self* or another) your sins are retained, for the power to free your*self* and all mankind is within you.

My next door neighbor was having trouble with her feet. The toes were so sensitive to touch she was unable to cover her feet at night, as even a sheet caused her pain. A woman in her 80's, raised in the Jewish faith, she went to doctor after doctor and followed all of their instructions to no avail. When I asked her what she wanted, she laughingly replied, "I'll settle for a new pair of feet." Then she agreed to forgive her*self* and together we imagined her saying, "My feet are fine, they are just like new."

That night she went to bed and fell asleep repeating this affirmation. Night after night she persisted in affirming her healthy feet and then, early one morning, something caused her to awaken. The bedside clock registered three, yet the room was as light as day. A man was standing at the foot of her bed, and as she watched, he took off her right foot and replaced it with a new one. Then he took off the left one and replaced it, smiled and vanished out of her sight. Rejoicing, she rose from her bed and walked through the house on her brand new feet. From that day forward her feet gave her no pain. The open sores healed and remained so for the rest of her life with us. She proved to her*self* that she had the power to forgive her sins, and that when she forgave them, her sins were forgiven. And so can you.

Your garment of flesh was woven by the seed of woman and it is dead. Although invisible, the inner you is the son of God who makes your garment alive. It can be seen, but your invisibility is more real than anything visible on earth. Everything responds to your imagination. If you want the world to change, all you have to do is change your thinking. Nothing exists outside of your imagination; therefore, nothing lives independent of your perception of it. Practice the art of forgiveness. Change your attitude towards a friend and watch him change, for your friend only exists in the "I" of you, the beholder. Listen carefully to your inner thoughts, for that is where your friend is created.

On December 25th the world celebrates the birth of Christ as an advent that took place nearly 2000 years ago, but Christ, the power and wisdom of God, walks this earth in the form of every being in it. Your garment was born from your mother's womb, but when Christ is born in you, he will come from your brain. His birth will take place in you, individually, for God (your own wonderful human imagination) cannot fail to individualize him*self*. Cut off your arms and legs, remove your organs and transplant your heart, but it is impossible for you to stop imagining.

Read the 23rd and 40th chapters of Psalms and put the word "Imagination" in the place of "LORD" and you will discover where your enemies are. Matthew says, "A man's enemies are those of his own household." (M't 10:36) Fear, doubt, limitation, anger, frustration, all of these are enemies and the cause of sin. Limiting your*self* to the evidence of your senses imprisons you, but imagination has the power to set you free. Imagine you are elsewhere and no power on earth can stop you from being there, for who can stop God? You can go anywhere you want to go, do anything you want to do and be anything you want to be when you let go of limitation, doubt and fear, for nothing is impossible to imagine.

Divine imagination created this world as a stage and filled it with objects that have no life. Being the ONLY reality, God entered his concept of you and turned your dead body into a living soul. Containing the whole, God sacrificed him*self* on your skull and fell asleep to make you alive, for it is God who dreams your life into being.

Imitate God by claiming you are now the person you would like to be. Give your friends what they would like to have by being conscious of their possession of it. You have the power to make the world beautiful or ugly, for the world is forever responding to your state of consciousness. Become conscious of beauty and beauty will preside, for as you perceive life to be, it is. And if you forgive the sins of another, they are forgiven, but if you retain them, they are retained. What a responsibility. The evidence of the senses holds man in bondage, but imagination sets all men free. Imagine and let it be for, marvelously resourceful, imagination has ways and means to bring all things to pass.

There is no such thing as karma, for you are God, individualized. You never were and never will be any other than your I-ness. Your Father made you, and chose you by becoming the being you are at the present time. Whatever pain or joy you have gone through, are going through or will go through, is experienced by your heavenly Father, for his I-ness has been, is being, and will always bear your cross.

As imagination, you have the power to create and the power to change that which is created. Memory built your world. If your memory is beautiful, beauty presides, but if it is ugly, ugliness is perpetuated. If change is desired, it must be done in your memory, for only as your thinking changes will your world be changed.

Everything is dependent upon your perception of it, for the world is forever responding to your thoughts. Forgive the sins of another by changing your thoughts of him and he is forgiven. But if you do not change your thoughts, you have retained his sins, for only as you forgive are you forgiven. Now I ask you to "Go forth and sin no more." (John 8:11)

## GOD, PLUS FAITH

**"Without faith, it is impossible to please him."**
**(Heb 11:6)**

God, your own wonderful human imagination, is the reality out of which you fashion your world, and all things are possible to him. Learn to believe in your invisible reality. Have faith in *self*, for without faith in your imagination it is impossible to please God.

Matthew tells the story of a rich young man who wanted to enter the kingdom of heaven. Told to sell all that he had and believe in *self*, he turned away because he had so many other beliefs. Seeing this Jesus said, "It is easier for a camel to pass through the eye of a needle than for a rich man to enter heaven." When asked, "Who can be saved?" Jesus answered, "With men who do not *know* the Lord's name it is impossible, but with God all things are possible." (M't 19:16-26) The rich man believed in the reality of the moment and the worldly pleasures of the day. Believing in the power of his wealth and earthly possessions, he did not believe in *self*, and therefore did not know the Lord's name. This name was revealed to Moses who heard the words, "I

AM, that is who I AM. That is my name forever, and by this name I shall be known throughout all generations." (Ex 3:13-15) To be aware is to mentally say I am and that is imagination.

Begin now to trust your awareness, for God, plus faith, is the sole cause of the phenomena of life. "Faith is the assurance of things hoped for; the evidence of things not seen. By faith the world was created by the word of God so that things which are seen were made out of things that do not appear, and without faith it is impossible to please him." (Heb 11:1-3,6) "He calls a thing which is not seen as though it were and the unseen becomes seen." (Rom 4:17, Catholic)

Your imagination (thought) can call a thing that is not seen and create that which is seemingly impossible. Knowing what you want, do not question its possibility; just call that which is not seen by imagining a scene as though it were. Move into your creation by giving it sensory vividness. Fix it by rejoicing in its reality. Then walk in its assumption and that which has been unseen by mortal eye will become seen.

God, your imagination, will never fail you as long as you have faith. All things are possible to you, for there is nothing impossible to imagine. All you need is a vivid imagination, a clear idea of what you want and a determinate vision of its fulfillment. Then, because God has ways you know not of, imagination will bring it to pass.

The Bible teaches, invites and encourages you to exercise your imagination, lovingly, on behalf of everyone and everything in the world. There is no external god, for God literally took upon him*self* the limitation and restriction of your body. It is he who is subject to all of your weaknesses. We are all that one God, buried in this fragmented state called humanity. If you know what you want and are willing to assume it, fall asleep hearing your friends' congratulations. Thank them.

Accept the fact before it is seen, and that which is now unseen by others will be seen. Everything in the world exists in your imagination, but you must call it into being. Although unseen by others, call your desire as though it were, and it will be seen by all.

A state of consciousness is like a city. Leave a city but it, like poverty, will remain for anyone to occupy. Feel sorry for your*self* and you have entered a state. Rejoice because of your good fortune and you leave the state of *self*-pity and enter the state of fulfillment. All states are permanent fixtures of the universe. Do not condemn a man for the state he is in, rather move him out by thinking of him in another. Nothing is impossible when you know how to imagine. You can go anywhere and anytime. You will discover that travel is not the privilege of the rich but of the man of imagination.

A state does not mind whether you enter it or not, nor does it care how long you stay. Your heart's desire is a state that you can enter by simply catching and assuming its mood. Would it make you happy? Then assume happiness, for that mood, sustained, will lead you to your heart's desire. Do not limit your dreams by your present state, for the occupant of a state of fabulous wealth is God—the same being as you. Always believing ahead of your evidence, catch the mood and you will believe the state of wealth into your world.

Everything which is now real was first imagined. The clothes you wear, your home and car were preceded by an imaginal act in the depths of your being before they came to the surface. Man had to first imagine going to the moon before he could conceive of the means to get there. You have to imagine before anything can become a fact. Man, not controlling his thinking, feeds his imagination negative thoughts and creates a hell on earth. The morning's paper will confirm this. But if you will control your thinking and feed your imagination positive, fulfilled thoughts, you will have a heaven on earth.

Then one day you will know who you really are. Jesus is not a myth but a glorious concept of truth. Buried in your skull and called imagination, he is the only reality. Begin now to loosen your thoughts and claim you are the God of scripture. Learn to believe in your own wonderful human imagination and feed it thoughts of love. You can create a world of love and peace, health and happiness while your are fulfilling all of your desires. All you need is God, plus faith!

## WHERE DO YOU LIVE?

**"Be ye transformed by the renewal
of your mind."      (Rom 12:2)**

Your state of consciousness determines the conditions and circumstances of your life. Look around and you will see the state in which you now live. If you do not like what you see, you can change it by seeing something different. This is done by thinking from a new idea. It is not easy to mentally walk away from your present, accustomed thoughts, because they have become habitual. But if you will persist, a new life will be yours.

A few years ago a very sordid cartoon appeared in the "New Yorker." Pictured was a small, disheveled room, with a sink full of dirty dishes. A middle-aged woman, wearing dirty clothes and matted hair, was sitting at a table reading a letter from her son. Her husband sat beside her. His clothes were torn and his feet, propped upon the table, exposed holes in his socks. The caption read: "He says he's homesick." Occupying rooms, your thoughts are as dirty dishes and unwashed cups within you and, through habit, it is easy to become homesick for these sordid rooms. But we are told to, "Cleanse the

inside of the cup that the outside also may be clean."
(Matt 23:26)

A state of consciousness is the sum total of all that
you believe, accept and consent to as true. What you
believe need not be true, it could be false, a half truth, a
lie, a superstition or a prejudice, but your belief is the
house in which you live, and as long as you remain
there similar problems will confront you. A physical
move will not change the circumstances of your life, for
you must change your thinking to change your world.
The Bible calls states of consciousness mansions of the
Lord, cities, rooms, and is always encouraging one to
move into the upper or higher level of *self.*

Want to know the state you are now in? Listen to
your thoughts, for they are always singing their own
song. Listen carefully, and you will hear the cause of life
reveal it*self* in your inner speech. If you have never
uncritically observed your reactions to life; if you are
totally unaware of your subjective behavior, then you
do not know the cause of your world. Forever standing
in the presence of infinite and eternal energy from which
all things proceed, your thoughts, following a definite
track, cause the energy to move out and crystallize
it*self.* Change your thoughts by transforming and
renewing your mind with new ideas, and you will
change your world.

Where do you live? Listen! Are you hearing your*self*
make negative comments? Are you excusing delay or
failure, arguing or condemning? Man has a peculiar
affection for feeling unwanted or hurt so he can talk
about it. Try to pull your*self* out of your present
habitual state and move into the house of your dreams.
Persist and it, too, will become a habit and externalize
it*self* in your world.

There is no one to change but *self.* If you dislike
another or think he dislikes you, the cause is yours.

Search your thoughts of him and you will find they were never pleasant. But if you will lay new thinking tracks he will appear to change. Persist and you will be transformed in spirit, for as you become conscious of what you seek, it is found. But if you do not persist until your thoughts are habitual, your former state will return. Then your world will remain just as it is, for your outer world changes only as it is inwardly directed to do so.

Joy and sorrow, peace and harmony, trouble and pain are caused by the use (or misuse) of your mind and speech. Awaken to a loving imagination and you will see everything subjectively related to your*self*. You will realize that the stranger had no power to come into your world. You, and you alone, drew him out of your*self*.

My friend Marilyn felt wronged. Her husband had confessed that he had been having affairs for over a year. He was sorry and promised not to repeat his acts, but Marilyn was hurt. Could she believe him? Could she ever trust him again? Her first impulse was to take their small child and leave, but then another thought began to worm its way into her mind. What if she had an affair! That night Marilyn went to bed consumed with the idea. Using her five senses she imagined and imagined until she fell asleep feeling the joy of revenge. The next day the thought would not leave her alone. It plagued her everywhere she went and the next night she repeated her imaginal act. During the morning of the third day a neighbor came to call. He was a man Marilyn had known for years; a husband, father, and friend of the family. But this time he said, "Marilyn, I think you are very desirable and I would like to have an affair with you." Shocked, she said, "I'll have to think it over," and after a short conversation he left.

Where did the neighbor come from? He had been a friend for years, yet had never approached her before.

Marilyn wanted an affair and, although she did not consciously say, "I want it to be *this* man" her neighbor had no power to come into her world save she call him out of her*self*. Marilyn is blessed, for she realized what she had done. Now she knows that thoughts have the power to create or destroy a world.

You can create a world of peace and harmony if you will but live in the state of Jesus Christ. This is done by making a conscious effort of guiding your thinking by love. Use your imagination to predetermine what you want to see and hear. Stop passively surrendering to appearances and put Christ to the test, for he is your wonderful imagination and the only power in the world.

Revision is so very important. Before retiring every night review your day and change any portion of it you do not want to repeat. My friend Peg has mastered the art of revision. Here is her story. As Peg was preparing for work she noticed a diamond was missing from her wedding band. Examining the ring more closely she began to imagine the sparkle and beautiful light reflections the diamond emanated. With her imaginary hands she ran her index finger across the band and felt the diamond and the security of the prongs. Placing the band on her dresser she drove to work, glancing often at her finger to view the diamond sparkle in the sunlight. This act she repeated many times during the day.

That night, before retiring, Peg brushed her teeth and just "happened" to look over her shoulder. Spotting something glistening on the bathroom rug she reached down and picked up her diamond which had been waiting there for her discovery. Now it is back in her ring and just as beautiful as ever . . . just as she always knew it was!

What would you have done if you were Peg? Would you have acted or reacted? Would you have accepted the missing diamond as final with no hope of being found, or would you have changed the facts as my friend did? "You must be a doer of the word and not a hearer only. For if you are a hearer and not a doer you are like a man who sees his face in the mirror, turns and straightway forgets what manner of man he is. But if you are a doer you are blessed with the deed, for as you look into the law of liberty you liberate yourself." (James 1:22-25) My friend liberated herself by seeing the diamond in her ring. Most people, through habit, would stew, fume and fret all day and retire allowing the sun to descend upon their wrath. But now that you know how to free yourself, I hope you will do it, for if you do not rewrite yesterday's events they will become tomorrow's problems.

Time and space cannot change the conditions of your life by themselves, for space is only the facility for experience and time the facility for change. You must become the operator of your powerful imagination. If you do not your life will never change.

Whenever you blame another, or try to justify failure, you are displaying your own dirty dishes and betraying your*self*. Stop condemning your*self*, for that is what you do when you condemn another. Instead, enter the kingdom of heaven by hearing your friend share his good news. Hold your head high and accept his congratulations. The kingdom of heaven, within you, can be entered any moment of time. Your friend may be thousands of miles away but, by imagining, you have given him a heavenly blessing which will cause a change in the structure of his mind.

Where do you live? I hope it is always in the feeling of fulfillment, for if you know who you are you know the world is yours and all within it. But knowledge alone is not enough. You could know everything there is to know about food, yet die of starvation if you do not eat. You are the eternal energy of the world. Become transformed by the renewal of your mind by being conscious of that which you seek. Live in that consciousness and you will find it!

"Faith is the assurance of things hoped for, the conviction of things not seen. By faith we understand that the world was created by the word of God, so that what is seen was made out of things which do not appear."      (Heb 11:1,3)

Faith is an abandonment of *self*, and scriptural faith is faith in God, who is love. Learn to yield to this presence of love within you. Have faith in *self*, for by him all things are made, and without him was not anything made that is made.

If you need money (and who doesn't), think of a scene which would imply you have it. Then yield to this being of love and fall asleep in the knowledge that he heard you. That he saw your act and will execute it. Walk as though you have plenty. Commit your*self* completely to the depth of your own being and allow him to externalize it for you. He tells you, "Your ways are not my ways. As the heavens are higher than the earth, so are my ways higher than your ways." (Isa 55:8,9) Do not question how you are going to get the money. Simply have faith, for He has ways and means you, on this surface level, know not of. Do this, and you will rise under compulsion to go through a series of events which will lead you to the fulfillment of your desire. Simply assume it is done. Commune with your *self* and give thanks that you have plenty, and it will be so.

Learn the mystery of faith, for God makes all things, good, bad and indifferent, through faith. Everything in eternity exists and man, as part of the eternal structure of the universe, exists. He did not grow out of a worm as our evolutionists believe. Evolution is confined to the affairs of man, but not to the creation of God. A hoe has been replaced by a tractor; a raft by a boat. A sail was added, then steam and now nuclear energy. That is evolution in the affairs of man, but not in the creation of God, for man is, and all things exist as an eternal part of the structure of the universe. "Eternity exists and all things in eternity independent of creation which was an act of mercy." (Wm. Blake) When God said, "Let us make man in our image" (Gen 1:26) man existed. God did not say, "Let us make something and call it man" he made you in his image. Then he became you. God had to lose all memory of his power in order to take upon himself the weakness and the limitation of your body. As you, he is forming him *self* into his own likeness. Raising that which he became, he redeems everything in the world.

While here you can be, or have, anything you desire. Just think about it. Where would you be and what would you be doing? Do not see your*self* doing it, but become involved in the doing. Yield to the depth of your own being and fall asleep in the assumption you have achieved your goal. Then relax in the knowledge that the depth of your being will externalize it for you. Tomorrow you may find your*self* doing things you had not planned to do, meeting the right people and being at the right place at the right time for your assumption to be externalized. That is how God creates.

"Commune with your own *self* upon your bed and be

silent." (Ps 4:4) Being aware, you are mentally saying "I am." That is your *self* and there is no other God. Your *self* is invisible, for you cannot see your thoughts as you can objects in space, yet your thoughts are the cause of your world. The day will come when you will see your true *self* as the Ancient of Days. Radiating love, he is your true identity and the only reality. It is your *self* that kills and makes alive, wounds and heals, and none can deliver out of his hands. If your thoughts are evil, imagination *(self)* will execute them for you, as there is no other creator. You are free to think what you like but remember, when you think, yield to your true *self* in faith, and it will be done for you.

We are told that, "The spirit of the Lord will not turn back until he has executed and accomplished the intents of his mind. In the latter days you will understand it clearly." (Jer 23:20) God intended to transform you into him*self* and he will not turn back until his purpose has been accomplished. You are the eloheim who came down from heaven and assumed the limit of contraction called man. Living in a world of shadows, a predetermined plan, called Jesus Christ, will unfold within you and God will have fulfilled his word.

God's promise is yours and it is irrevocable, but the law requires faith. When you know what you want, construct a scene which would imply its fulfillment and enter into it. Feel its reality and give thanks to the depth of your *self*. Fall asleep confident that he heard you and will execute it for you. Have faith in your own wonderful human imagination, for whatever your desire may be, it came from your heavenly Father. Yield completely to him and have faith, for nothing is impossible to God.

It costs you nothing to imagine. "Come, buy wine, buy milk without money." (Isa 55:1) What does it cost to have faith in God? Imagine, and walk in faith, knowing that the depth of your being has ways your surface

*The Invisible You*

mind knows not of. Do not try to tell your Father how to do it; simply leave it in his hands. Give thanks and have faith in *self*, for there is nothing in the world but *self*.

## THE MAN OF IMAGINATION

**"In your limbs lie nations twain, rival races from their birth. One of the mastery will gain, the younger over the elder reign."**
**(Gen 25:23)**

The room you are now in, and its contents, are perceived by the sense man, for he sees objects as present in the outer world. His younger brother, called imagination, sees objects which are not present, yet sense perceived. These two men are rival races from their birth, but the Lord from heaven, who is your own wonderful human imagination, is destined to rule the outer, physical you. Your body of flesh and blood is only a state of consciousness, but your imagination is immortal. It is he who plays the part of the rich man, poor man, beggar and thief, doctor, lawyer, merchant, chief. The part he plays is up to you, for his name forever and ever is I am.

Several years ago our house was in desperate need of a new roof. My husband was unemployed at the time, and the only way we could afford one was in our imagination. So we stood in front of the house and let our "younger man" see a new roof and heave a sigh of relief because it was paid for. Physically we were in the state of poverty, and our bank account proved it true, but our inner man owned the world, so we let him pay for the roof.

During that period of time our house had a large cement patio which needed to be covered. Knowing exactly what I wanted, I called my man of imagination into being and saw beautiful plants hang from the patio roof. Sat with friends and heard them proclaim its beauty as I watched the sunlight dance through the bamboo shades. Then I returned to my man of sense and the responsibilities of the day.

Twenty-five years ago my husband gave me a Singer portable sewing machine as a wedding present. One day, while idly mending a torn sleeve, I pretended I was using a new zig-zag machine. There was nothing wrong with my old one, but it would be fun to have a new machine in a beautiful stationary cabinet. My mind traveled from room to room as I searched for its perfect location, and then I dismissed the thought.

During this period of my life I was attending Neville's lectures and would carry my heavy Wollensak recorder to and from his meetings, always imagining it was a new, lightweight Sony. And when my husband's new shoes hurt his feet, I imagined comfortable ones. Imagination was fun and cheap, and I was willing to test its reality.

Working in an office five days a week I rarely came home for lunch, but this day I did. Seeing the front door open, I walked into the house and knew at once that we had been robbed. Everything movable had been taken, even my sewing machine, tape recorder and my husband's new shoes. At the time it seemed as though fate had dealt us a bitter blow, but one month later our insurance company gave us enough money for a new zig-zag sewing machine, a Sony tape recorder, the camera of my husband's dreams and even a new pair of shoes for his feet. There was also plenty of money for the new roof and patio cover. I did not know how I was going to get the things I desired, I simply assumed I had them. My assumption caused men, living in the state of a thief, to enter our house and take that which was not theirs. They performed their act so that my desires would be fulfilled.

There are infinite states in this world, and if you know what you want and claim you have it, every state necessary to make your desire come true will appear the moment you need it. "God made everything for its purpose, even the wicked for the day of trouble." (Prov 16:4) Therefore, I do not condemn the thief who played a part in my life, for he is not to blame. He chose the part, but I was the actor of the play. And who am I? The younger man, the man of imagination, for I conceived an idea and executed it by thinking it was real.

We are all viewing our world from a state of consciousness. You are in one right now, and if you do not like what is taking place you can move into another. Any state can be occupied by your consciousness, as the occupant of one state does not differ from the occupant of any other. All states are called forth and made real with God's name. Just say "I am wealthy" and you have called forth the state of wealth. But an idea (desire) in itself produces nothing. Only as the desire is felt will it awaken motor actions and become effective. Being wealthy is an idea, but feeling wealthy is reality. Imagination, spiritual sensation, is the creative you. Feel the reality of a desire and it will be yours. Churchill once said, "The mood determines the fortunes of people rather than the fortunes, the mood." Your mood, your desire felt, always precedes your fortune.

Esau and Jacob's story is one of *self*-deception through feeling. Esau, the elder, was covered with hair and, therefore, real to the outer world while Jacob, the younger, was hairless and unreal. Isaac, the father of all life, was deceived. Feeling his son Jacob (his inner desire) had the reality of fulfillment, he believed in its birth, thereby giving desire the right to be born. A rose, though not physically present, can be real through Jacob, for you can feel its soft velvet leaves, smell its fragrance and see its beauty in your imagination. A friend need not be present for you to hear his voice or touch his hand in thought. You can even taste the salt air of the sea while living in the Sahara desert, for nothing is impossible to Jacob, the man of imagination in you.

Begin to recognize this dual being within you and learn to let the younger one reign. The elder sees only the fact that you owe more than your bank account shows. Let Jacob put in fifty times more. Do not be concerned as to how it is going to get there, for the man of imagination has ways and means the sense man knows not of. When Isaac felt the reality of Jacob he gave him the right of birth. Feel a huge bank account is now yours, and its birth will appear in your world.

As a man of sense you are of the earth and to dust you will return. But the younger you is the Lord from heaven. As your imagination, he is embodied in your body of flesh and blood. It is there that he dreams your dream of life. Learn to trust no one but him, for he is the creative one in you who will awaken one day, and when he does you are God Him*self*.

**"Well done good and faithful servant, you have been faithful over a few things, now I will make you a ruler over many."** (Matt 25:21)

Your thoughts, like rambling sheep, need a shepherd. Become the good shepherd and master your thoughts. Rule your mind and you will rule the world.

The kingdom of heaven is said to be like a man who, before starting his journey, called his servants together and gave them property. One received five talents, another two, and still another one, each according to his ability. When the master returned and learned that the one who had been given five had increased it to ten he said, "Well done good and faithful servant, you have been faithful over a few things, now I will make you a ruler over many." The servant given two had increased it to four and was also highly commended. But when the master learned that the servant who had been given one had buried it, he condemned him and gave his talent to the one who had ten. (Matt. 25)

Your thoughts determine your talents and every day they are used according to your ability. Are you prejudiced? Superstitious? Filled with doubt and fear? Or do you believe you are the cause and creator of life, with the power to change it? If you do, you have received one, two or five talents, according to your ability. But a talent, like a muscle that has not been exercised, sleeps and atrophies. Understanding the law of assumption will not produce results. The law must be used in order for your talents to be made alive.

The Lord told Amos, "I will not destroy the house of Jacob. But I will shake the house of Israel among all nations as one shakes with a sieve yet no pebble shall fall upon the earth." (Amos 9:9) Jacob is he who lives in the house of Israel and, although scattered, your Israel is what you want. Do not look on the outside for another to give it to you, for not one pebble of hope shall fall upon the earth. Rather, see its fulfillment in your mind, for your desire is a part of Israel that is scattered. Form love, peace and harmony in your womb (your mind) by becoming a perfect servant and bring Jacob to the Lord.

A sick friend is brought to Israel by clothing him with the skins of Esau. Deceive your heavenly Father into believing your friend is healthy. Your wish is smooth skinned, but it can be clothed with the hair of Esau by the use of your talents. If you can only use one of your five senses, use one, but if you practice your talents will increase abundantly.

Jacob is lost in the minds of men. Become a good and faithful servant of the Lord and clothe Jacob with perfection. But, if you know how to clothe him and do not do it, you are the servant who buried his talent. Believe in your imagination and watch your thoughts project themselves on the screen of space. Then, having been faithful over a few things, you will become a ruler over many and your true identity will be revealed. The world claims you are a little spermatozoa. If that were true your end would be spermatozoa for all ends run true to origin. But your origin is God; therefore your end is God.

Make a vivid and lifelike picture of what you would see if your desire were physically present. Enter your house of Israel and see it with the eyes of Jacob. Consciously occupy your picture and you have brought Jacob to the Lord.

> "If one would only advance confidently in the direction of his dream, endeavoring to live the life he has imagined, he will meet with success unexpectedly." (Wm. Blake)

You have the power to confer reality on a wish; therefore, you have the power to bless or curse your*self* or friend. Use your talent of sound and hear your friend tell you he is fine. Assume he embodies the state of health. Walk faithful to that thought and your friend will transform his image in your mind. Then you are truly blessed, for the one you have transformed is your*self*.

Israel is made up of the ideas that float in your mind. Shepherd your thoughts and become their king. Command an idea to clothe it*self* in form and you will make it real. "Is-real" is the true Israel. Become the perfect servant. Start now to discipline your thoughts and rule your mind.

Jesus called Peter "Simon" which means "to hear." When questioned, "Simon, lovest thou me?" he is saying, "Do you love what you hear your*self* saying?" Then feed your sheep by ruling your thoughts and walking faithful to an invisible state. Do not bury Simon, but take your talent of hearing and prove you love what you say in that inner sanctum of *self*.

Jacob, your subjective state, is a smooth skinned lad. Add the hair, or external reality of Esau, and your subjective state will take on the appearance of reality.

Detach your thoughts from the state and its corresponding external witness will fade. Surrounded by success you can detach your mind from it by thinking of failure. Persist and failure will take over to prove that success was not on the outside at all. Success gave the appearance of reality while it was clothed, but it was only the shadow whose light was an idea with which you were identified.

Remember, nothing is ever lost. It is simply scattered in Israel. Feel you possess that which is seemingly gone. Remain faithful to your assumption and you will find it. Clothe all of your desires in reality through the use of your five talents. Bring every desire of your heart to your heavenly Father, your consciousness and he will give them the right of birth.

An external fact is not truth, for its reality is in your assumption. Truth does not depend upon fact, but upon the intensity of your imagination. Jesus, representing the truth, faced Pilate, the epitome of fact, and would not answer when Pilate asked, "What is truth?" Fact believes a thing must be externally real to be true, but the truth that sets you free is the knowledge that all reality is in the mind. Truth and fact always oppose one another. But if you will disentangle your*self* from the state you are now conscious of, it will cease to be, for a state must have consciousness to be alive. Appropriate a state. Embody it with consciousness and all that the state represents is yours.

Start with one talent and increase it to two, then five, ten and even twenty until you are worthy of being a friend. Then, having been faithful in a few things, you will be made Lord over many. Once a slave to external reality, begin to serve others by the use of your talents and you will learn how to walk as a friend. Commune with your deeper *self* as though he is another. Talk across invisible states as a man speaks face to face with a friend. Do this and you will see the face of God's only Son, David, for he is your true *self* reflected back.

God the Father embodied himself in the consciousness of you in the hope that you would awaken to your true being. This is done through the process of being the servant, the friend and finally David, God's only begotten Son who is one with his Father and the ruler of the mind.

## PRUNING SHEARS

**"He appeared to put away sin by the sacrifice of *self*."** (Heb 9:26)

T he pruning shears of revision are magic, for with them you can turn sickness into health, sorrow into joy and poverty into unlimited wealth. And their daily use will awaken the spirit of Jesus, in you, which is the continual forgiveness of sin.

Scripture tells us that the sinner should always go free. Learn to forgive and you will never again condemn, but set your fellow man free by forgiveness. Forgive by identifying every man with the state you would like to embody. Do for him what you would like him to do for you. Discard no man, but redeem him, and your*self*, by seeing the seeming other express the ideal you want to externalize. This is the process by which your redemption is brought about.

God placed man in the garden of Eden to dress it and to keep it. That garden is your mind. It, like every garden, needs to be pruned of the weeds of wrong thinking which reveal themselves as the conditions and circumstances of your life. Your garden is projected on the screen of space. Look carefully and you will see what you have allowed to grow. You did not come here to amass a fortune, be famous or powerful, but simply to tend your garden, for you were placed there to dress it and keep it filled with lovely growth.

Every being in the world is rooted in you and cannot bear anything other than the nature you, the root, allow. Change can only be brought about by changing the source (the cause) of what has grown. "See yonder fields? The sesamum was sesamum, the corn was corn, the silence and the darkness knew and so is a man's fate born." (Unknown) Do not judge another but turn within and prune your thoughts of him with the pruning shears of revision.

When retiring at night, review your day. Think of the conversations, the events and meetings you experienced. Then rewrite those events as you wish they had happened. After rewriting the script, relive your revised day until you feel it actually happened. Do this and you will realize that freedom and forgiveness are indissolubly linked, for you cannot be free and not forgive. Imagination is he who binds and condemns, and imagination is in you. Judge another and you are anchored by your judgment. But, by identifying another with the ideal you want to realize, you free your*self.* "Forgive and you shall be forgiven" (Lu 6:37) is true and so is the reverse, for if you do not forgive you shall not be forgiven. Why? Because all things spring forth from you, the one beholding it.

Practice the art of repentance and the spirit of truth will arouse it*self* within you. Then you will understand the words in the Book of Hebrews, "He appeared to put away sin by the sacrifice of *self*." (Heb 9:26) The *self* of man is the sum total of all that he believes and consents to as true. This *self* must be sacrificed. The knowledge that a lady desires to be happily married becomes a part of your *self*. Sacrifice that *self* by claiming "She is as happily married as I am." Do that and you will sin no more, but realize your every goal in life.

You are, in reality, all that you consent to, accept and believe to be true. Do you believe your neighbor is unemployed and cannot find a job? Then put away his sin by hearing him tell you of his fantastic job and salary. Do you know someone who is ill? Bring him before your mind's eye and see him as a healthy, happy spirit. Commune with him and believe in his reality. Do the work which you were sent to do for you are responsible for every being you meet.

A blind man sees the world objective to and therefore detached from him*self*. You are not blind, but asleep. As you revise you awaken to the realization that everything is subjectively related to *self*. So do not discard anyone, for your life is the process by which you redeem your *self*. This is done by using the pruning shears of revision.

With God all things are possible. Dreaming your world into being you have the power to wake from sleep. You are the habitation of every created thing and by you all things are made, and without your consciousness is not anything made that is made. Begin now to raise everyone in your world, for as you raise another you raise your*self*. Moving upward on an infinite vertical line, you save your*self* only as you save another. Prune your mind, your tree of life, and become a loving, conscientious gardener in the garden of God.

## SEEDS OF DESIRE

**"Be not deceived, God is not mocked as a man sows, so shall he reap."**
**(Gal 6:7)**

A s long as the earth endures there will be seedtime and harvest, for all things must bring forth after their kind. This is the law, the law of identical harvest. The earth is your mind (your imagination) and the seeds planted there are ideas. All things exist in your mind and, although people and places appear outside of you, their reality is within. There is an art in the use of this law and, like all arts, it takes practice to use it wisely. Suppose you want a better job, but have been told you are not qualified and the job can never be yours. Can you use the law to get it? Yes, if you plant your seed of fulfilled desire. Here is what you do.

Ignore the world and ask your*self*, "What do I want?" Then, assume you have it. If you want to be the boss, sit behind his desk. Park your car in his space. Hear the other employees greet you with respect. Feel the importance of your position, and persist. From the moment you sit in the chair and feel the solidity of the desk in front of you, do not allow your thoughts to deny your position. If you will discipline your mind, and think from the new idea you have just planted, your outer world will rearrange it*self* and you will have your job. This I promise, for the reality of this world is in your imagination. Its actuality is that which is projected in space.

The room you are now in is real, is it not? You can see its objects, touch the chairs and walls, walk on the floor and feel its cubic reality. Yet the adjoining room, which you left only a moment ago, is now only a flat picture. Why? Because you give a room reality when you enter it. You are all imagination and, as such, you must be wherever you are in imagination. Wearing your body as you do a suit of clothes, you will discard it one day, but your imagination will live forever.

Start now and learn to invest your time by your conscious use of the law. Learn to be aware of what you are thinking, because the law will not allow you to deceive your*self*, as you are reaping your imaginal acts morning, noon and night. You may not remember when a seed was planted, but you cannot harvest that which you have not sown. Read the paper and react and you have planted a seed. Condemn another and, because he only exists in your imagination, you are condemning your*self*. Every time you read a magazine, watch television or hear the news on the radio you are putting ideas in your mind; ideas that must come to harvest, so be ever watchful and aware of what you are thinking, for as you sow you must reap.

Imagination can make you what you want to be and take you any place you want to go if you will not limit your*self*. Just plant the seeds of fulfilled desires in your mind and watch for their fulfillment. Not everything takes months or years to grow, some things come up overnight. Don't be impatient and dig up your seed tomorrow to see if it is growing. Simply accept the joy of possession and in its own good time your seed will come to fruition in your world.

There are many obligations to life which must be met. Rent must be paid, clothes bought, food and transportation paid for, so use the law by praying for them. "And when you pray, believe that you receive it, and you will." (Mk 11:24) Pray by assuming you have what you want. Feel your*self* doing what you want to do; see what you want to see and be where you want to be. Plant your seed of desire with the feeling of possession until you explode within your*self*. When this happens energy has moved out of you and your seed will grow to maturity by externalizing it*self* in your world.

Learn to believe in your imagination, for you and your imagination are one. Test your*self* and imagine as great as it is possible for you to imagine. The only handicaps you possess are those you impose upon your*self*. Stop limiting God by limiting your*self*. You have the choice of the seeds you plant. Good or bad, their planting is entirely up to you. But if you will invest your seeds of desire, consciously, and watch them grow, they will blossom into fruiting in your world. If you want money, make money your seed. Do not be concerned as to how or from whom it comes, just live as though you had plenty and you will.

If you are in Los Angeles and would like to travel, sit in your chair and assume you are in New York City. If you are there would you see Los Angeles, or any other town, around you? Of course not. You would know that Los Angeles was three thousand miles to your west. Instead, surround your*self* with the tastes and smells, the sights and sounds of New York. Motion can be detected only by a change of position relative to an object. The object, in this case, is Los Angeles. You, the reality of all things, have changed position relative to

Los Angeles and have given it to New York City. That is how it is done.

You can do the same thing in your social, financial or intellectual world. Today your friends know you as a certain person. In your imagination let them see you as a social butterfly; a millionaire or an intellectual giant. Rearrange the structure of your mind and fall asleep in that assumption. You have now planted a new seed of thought and, since all things come forth after their kind, what you have imagined will appear in your world. But you cannot deceive yourself because God (your imagination) is not mocked. Your assumption is the seed and your mind the ground. Water your seed with persistence and fertilize it with feeling and your seed will grow to produce much fruit in your world.

It is possible to pray, not only for yourself, but for others. Job prayed for his friends and his own captivity was lifted. Pray for your friends by hearing their good news. Rejoice and feel the thrill of success, for feeling is a creative act, and as you feel you plant a seed. Where? In your imagination! Now, do you believe in God and that all things are possible to him? Then believe in your own wonderful human imagination for that is who God is. The fulfillment of your imaginal act has its own appointed hour to ripen and flower. If it seems long do not be disturbed, simply persist in your assumption and wait, for it is sure and it will not be late.

When I was first married I didn't want a child, not at first. But as the years flew by a desire began to stir within me for a baby of my own to love. The feeling persisted as the years went by, but no sign of pregnancy was mine. Then I began to imagine. Night after night I fell asleep holding my baby in my arms. During the day I fed him, changed his diapers, tucked him in for his nap and still had no signs of conceiving. Two years passed and one spring day I found myself in the hospital recovering from a total hysterectomy. Now hope was gone and there was nothing left to do but believe, yet how do you believe without hope? These were my doubts and fears as I called my sister-in-law to ask if she would stay with me when I arrived home from the hospital. It was then she told me of a friend. A friend whose daughter was going to have a baby in September and wanted to put it up for adoption.

The spark of desire was not dead. In fact it burst into flame and six months later a baby boy came into our home and our hearts and there he has remained for twenty-some odd years. Now I know nothing is impossible to possess if it is possible to imagine. And, although I imagine it here and now, its fulfillment is sure and will appear at its own appointed hour, for our son is the perfect son for us. We only had to imagine and then wait for him to arrive in our world.

I have always believed in God, but I learned to believe in the God in me. Do you believe your own wonderful human imagination is God? I hope you do, but if the word "God" conveys the sense of an existent something outside of you, you do not know "You are the temple of the Living God and the Spirit of God dwells in you." (1 Co 3:16) You are asked to "Test yourself and see. Do you not believe that Jesus Christ is in you? —unless, of course, you fail to meet the test (11 Co 13:5) Test him and you will find that God is in you *as* you. Call upon your own wonderful human imagination and you will know that the world is yours and all within it, for nothing will be impossible to you. You will simply plant your seeds and watch them grow in your world.

## COMMIT YOUR SPIRIT

**"Into thy hands I commit my spirit. Thou hast redeemed me, O Lord, faithful God."**
**(Ps 31:5)**

Crucifixion begins the drama of life. It is the end that begins all things, for you must die to what you are now, crucify and bury your consciousness in what you want to be, if you ever hope to taste the fruit of success. Commit your spirit into God's hands by dying to your old thoughts. Consciously create new ones from the assumption that your desire is real. Do not concern your*self* as to how it is going to come about; simply surrender your life into God's hands and He, in his infinite power and wisdom, will make it so.

Commit your*self* to any desire by the act of crucifixion. Surrender to the spirit of success, happiness, health, fame or fortune and you are committed. Quietly feel your dream has come true. Catch the mood and sustain it for a moment of unconsciousness. Do that and you have been crucified, dead and buried in that feeling. Then wait, for time will raise you from your dead state and you will ascend into your new one.

No matter where you go, or what you do, you cannot

get away from being aware, and you are crucified to that which you are aware of. If you are conscious of lack, crucify your*self* to the feeling of plenty. Bury your*self* in that feeling and you will rise from your grave wearing security's cross. Your Father's name is I am. Commit your spirit for money into His hands by feeling secure. There are only two characters in the Bible, God and his Son. Called David in the Old Testament and Christ in the New, God's Son is crucified, dead and buried in you. Symbolized as your power and wisdom, he is a man after your own heart. It is David who has done, is doing and will do all of your will regardless of the pain or sorrow it may cause. He will execute ignoble thoughts just as easily and as quickly as noble ones, for he is under compulsion to do your will.

Scripture has not and never will be fulfilled on earth, for God and his Son are within every individual. You are God's Son experiencing the fires of affliction here on earth. When the dross is burned away and only molten gold remains, David (the personification of your power and wisdom) will reveal you as his Father. Being all imagination, it is impossible to separate your power to imagine from imagination. As you cannot separate thought from *self*, you cannot separate your capacity to imagine from imagination for they are one.

"In the beginning was the Word and the Word was with God and the Word was God." (John 1:1) The Word is imagination and the power and wisdom to imagine. Jesus Christ means Father/Son. As the prodigal son you have gone astray, wasting your power and giving your wisdom away. But when the Holy Spirit brings all things to your remembrance, David will appear to show you that your power and wisdom has been restored.

In the New Testament Christ says, "I have come to do the will of him who sent me." (Joh 6:38) But in the

Book of Acts it is recorded that the Lord said, "I have found in David, the Son of Jesse, a man after my own heart who will do all my will." (Acts 13:22) Now, you cannot have a conflicting statement. If David will do all of God's will and Christ came to do his will are they not the same being? The 22nd Psalm begins, "My God, my God, why hast thou forsaken me?" and the 69th Psalm cries out, "Save me, O God" while the 53rd chapter of Isaiah asks the question, "Who has believed our report." These chapters are the foundations for the trials described in the New Testament. In the Old Testament David thought God had forgotten him, but Christ finds justification in the New.

Although you may not be able to pay your bills, you are the Lord, the creator of the universe. The world is yours to do with as you will. All you need to do is subjectively appropriate it. Let me illustrate my point by telling you about my neighbor. One day she lost her diamond broach. After she had torn the house apart, checked every closet and searched every drawer she came to see me. Sitting quietly in my home I asked her to describe her broach to me. Calling forth exact memory banks as to detail of shape, size, thickness, the number of diamonds and their location, we felt the broach and ran our fingers across the diamond's rough edges. Then she left, promising to go to sleep that night holding the broach in her hand. The next day, as she was preparing lunch, she felt the strangest urge to go to her closet and look at her black knit dress. She had checked that dress many times before, but the desire was so acute she stopped what she was doing and walked to the bedroom. Taking the black dress out of the closet she found the broach partially concealed under its collar.

My friend had subjectively appropriated her broach. She had buried herself in the feeling that it was now objectively real and fell asleep in that consciousness. While in the state of loss, the broach remained hidden from her view, but when she changed her thinking, that which was seemingly lost, was found. Her act was imaginal, not physical. Willing to commit her*self* into the hands of her Father, she subjectively appropriated her objective hope by feeling the broach.

Now, it is said that Noah's ark was built on three levels. The first, or physical, level reveals an ark with three floors and stairs leading upwards. The same thought, taken psychologically, would reveal *self* as the ark floating on a sea of illusion. But when you spiritually know you are the ark, you realize that everything you see, hear, taste, touch and smell is in you. That everything represents a state of consciousness and "I am" the occupant of every state. The arresting officer says I am and so does the prisoner. God is the judge and the victim, the murderer and the murdered, for he is the occupant of every state. You are God, traveling from state to state. Leave the state of ill health by giving it no consciousness. Then crucify your*self* on the state of health and as you bury your I am in it, health will rise to greet you in the morn.

It is possible to remain in a state for many years or get out of it in twenty-four hours, for every state is made alive by occupancy. Do not pity or feel sorry for another, for if you do your consciousness will cause the state to objectify it*self* in your world. And, if the state is unpleasant to another, it will be unpleasant to you when you join him there. Instead, emphathize by rejoicing in his new state and you have crucified him to it.

Faith is an act which is a negation of all activity, for in it God acts. Have faith in God by crucifying your*self* on the cross of your desire. Drown your*self* in the flood of emotion and you will rise to a new and completely fulfilled tomorrow, for you are God.

*The Invisible You*

**"Be ye doers of the Word and not hearers only, deceiving yourselves." (Ja 1:22)**

H ave you ever listened to your imagination? He is speaking to you every moment of time and creating your world by his word. Listen closely. Do you hear him speak words that are displeasing you, and you are doing nothing about them? Then you are a hearer only, deceiving your*self*. But when you change his words to those of your own choosing, you are a doer who looks into the perfect law of liberty and liberates him*self*. Learn to consciously guard your thoughts and you will no longer be a hearer who forgets, but a doer who acts and is blessed in the doing.

"God said to Moses, 'I will have mercy on whom I have mercy, and I will have compassion on whom I have compassion.' Will what is molded say to its molder, 'Why have you made me thus?' Has the potter no right over the clay to make out of the same lump one vessel for beauty and another for menial use?" (Rom 9: 15,20,21) You are the God spoken of here and your friend or enemy is the clay. You may have mercy or compassion upon him, but he cannot control your thoughts, for you are the potter of all life and nothing is independent of your perception of it.

Let me illustrate by telling you of a friend of mine who was a doer and not a hearer only. Believing that everything in the world is clay, he resolved to "remold" a vessel in his hand in the form of his 70-year old mother. She had had major surgery and was confined to a wheelchair for life. He did not expect his mother to change without help, so he began to carry on inner conversations with her from the idea that she was healthy and walking about the house. Guarding his thoughts, he congratulated her on her speedy recovery. Watched her walk toward him and even heard her tell him of the dance contest she had won. Being a doer he acted and is blessed in the doing, for today his mother is not only walking, but is actively involved in helping others do the same. So you see, we save ourselves as we save our fellowmen.

Your world is reflecting the activity of your imagination. You are its molder and if that which you have remolded does not change it is because you have not persisted. But if you become a doer and persevere, knowing that the clay cannot challenge you, you will be blessed in the doing. A man I know had a mole on his face which bled each time he shaved. Becoming a doer, he "reworked" his damaged clay by seeing his face free and clear of any blemish. Then one day, while shaving, he discovered the mole had vanished with no trace of its having ever been there before.

You are God, molding your world. If unemployed and you wish to be working, employment is your clay. Would you tell a friend of your new job? Then do it in your mind's eye. Persevere by occupying your new state and, depending upon your intensity, the new job will become your reality. Finding her*self* in a job she disliked intensely, my friend became a doer. Using her intensity she spent the day saying to her friends and associates, "I love my job." This she did in her imagination, and that night she was fired. Angry and frustrated, she left the job with an even greater resolve, and that night fell asleep conscious of her wonderful, highly fulfilling position. The next day, while visiting a friend, she met a man who needed an assistant, and is now working with people she respects, meeting challenges she enjoys and making more money than she ever dreamed possible. My friend saw the world as her clay, molded by her thoughts. Her world crumbled only to be remolded into its perfect shape as it seemed good for her, the potter, to do. Become the good potter. Change your thoughts by becoming a doer and not a hearer only and you will stop deceiving your*self*.

Can you imagine a state and see it harden into fact? Yes, if you persevere. God hardened Pharaoh's heart so that he had no choice in what he did. Think of my friend's mother as Pharaoh. The doctors, with their fixed belief in her inability to walk, hardened her heart. But my friend heard the message of mercy and his mother walks today. If there is something you want changed, change your fixed belief of it by imagining something different, for you have caused its heart to harden into fact. Persevere by controlling your thoughts. Force your*self* to think from the fulfillment of your desire and you will be blessed in this doing, for your world will change right before your eyes.

God's law was given to awaken you, the individual. Take your lump of clay, be it your*self* or a seeming other, and make of it anything you want. The mother was the same lump of clay, but transformed by the potter from a menial vessel into one of great beauty. You are the potter and do not differ from my friend or any other being in the world. Learn to play the game of life wisely, for you have within you the power to make the world conform to any image you desire.

Start now to refuse to accept anything that does not conform to your ideal image. See every individual as a piece of clay and you its creator. Do you have outstanding bills with no visible means of payment? Do not accept these facts, but pay them all with your imaginary money, for everything must first be imagined.

In every man's hand lies buried the universe that he may be able to feel a flower or a tree. The first letter of the Hebrew name of God is "yad" which means "hand." God gave you his hand which is capable of molding. Take your imaginary hand and feel the reality of your desire. Do what you would do if your wish were a reality. Become a doer of the word and not a hearer only. Look into the perfect law of liberty. Persevere and you will liberate your*self!*

## THE ART OF FORGIVENESS

**"Lord, how often shall my brother sin against me and I forgive him? Seventy times seven."**
**(Matt 18:21)**

I f you can distinguish the eternal human that walks among these stones of fire in bliss and woe, from the states in which the spirit travels, you will discover the art of forgiveness.

Many crimes may be committed in a play on Broadway, but you never condemn the actor because you know he is only following the script. The author put the words in his mouth and determined his actions. And so it is with your life. This world is a play, authored by God, and everyone in it is a state of consciousness playing their part. When you can discriminate between the state and its occupant, you will forgive everyone, for God wrote this fabulous play and every state belongs to him. The actor of a solidified state has a name, age and serial number, but the author is invisible. Learn to forgive everyone in your world, for he is only playing the part you, the author, have created.

Hold an image of a person in your mind's eye and it binds you, for that image is your*self*. And, "Whatever you bind on earth has been bound in heaven and what-ever you loose on earth has been loosed in heaven." (Matt 18:18) Think your friend is ill and you have bound him on earth and in heaven. Forgive him by thinking he is well, and you have released him from the state of illness both in heaven and on earth. When you forgive another you are, in truth, forgiving your*self* for the Father who forgives is *self*.

One night, in vision, I saw a match strike the earth which instantly burst into flame. Then a serpent emerged from the center of the flame and rose to stand erect in its midst. As I watched, its head became human and his arms stretched out on either side, as the serpent was transformed into a human cross placed in the center of raging flames.

You are that serpent wearing the cross of man. This world is a furnace and experience is the fire from which there is no escape. Depart this world and you are instantly restored to life. There to continue your journey until you are reduced to your true *self* which is liquid, molten gold. Then you will rise, as a fiery serpent, into the one body which is the one Spirit, one Lord, one God and Father of all.

Do not try to compare your mortal body with your immortal *self*, for you are planted in a physical body, but your spiritual body will rise. Planted in weakness, you rise in power. Planted in dishonor you rise in glory. There is only one being in the world. You are that one who left your heavenly home and entered this world of death to become individualized. One day you will return to your immortal body and then you will know your*self* to be the one who is God.

While wearing your cross you are creating your own flames by your thoughts, totally unaware that you are the cause of life. But the day will come when you will find that which was lost, and that is God Himself, the

*The Invisible You*

Father of all life.

"You can see from what I teach that I do not consider the just or the wicked to be in a supreme state, but to be everyone of them states of the sleep into which the soul may fall in its deadly dreams of good and evil." (Wm. Blake) Everyone is in a state of sleep. Learn to distinguish between the sleeping immortal and the state into which he has moved. Loving your dear ones, you would forgive them no matter what they did would you not? Extend your circle now to encompass your friends. Then make it larger and encompass those you do not know. Do this and you will realize there is only one being. That being is the one who says I am.

Practice the art of repentance by simply changing your thinking. Identify your friend with the state he would like to be in and, to the degree you are *self*-persuaded, his former state will become transformed and he will reflect your new thoughts of him for all the world to see.

In the earliest gospel we are told, "The kingdom of heaven is at hand; repent and believe in the gospel." (Mk 1:15) Change your thinking and believe the true story of Christianity. Then put it into practice. Christianity is the fulfillment of the promises Jehovah made to *self* (called Israel) through his servants, the prophets. When the story of Jesus Christ is reenacted in you, you will know you are Christ, for you will have fulfilled God's promise to Israel. Then you will forgive everyone, for you will know that everyone is your*self*.

**"Without faith it is impossible to please him."**      (Heb 11:6)

F aith does not give reality to unseen things—rather, loyalty to unseen reality gives meaning to faith! In this world reality, the cause of the phenomena of life, is not seen, so you are called upon to have faith. And "Faith is the assurance of things hoped for; the conviction of things not seen. By faith we understand that the world was created by the word of God so that what is seen was made out of things which do not appear." (Heb 11:1,2)

Scriptural faith is faith in your unseen reality who so loved you he became you. Imitate him. Fall in love with your unseen reality, for by him all things are made and without him was not anything made that is made. Knowing what you want, create a scene implying you already have it. Enter the scene and you have given it your reality. Then have faith in God, knowing he heard and saw your act, and will execute it for you. Paul's wonderful hymn of love, paraphrased, would read: "Though I speak in the tongues of men and angels; though I have the power of prophesy, understand all mysteries and have all knowledge; though I give away all that I have and give my body to be burned, if I have not faith I cannot please him." (1 Cor 13:1-3)

The surface of your being may claim your desire cannot be, but nothing is impossible to God. Commit your *self* to your fulfilled desire by feeling and acting as though you had it. Do that and you have commissioned God, the depth of your being, to externalize it for you. "His ways are not your ways and, as the heavens are higher than the earth, so are his ways higher than yours." (Isa 55:8,9) Do not question, simply yield to God and have faith. Commune with your true *self* and give thanks that it is finished, and it will be.

God makes all things, good, bad and indifferent, for everything man can imagine already is. Eternity exists, and all things in eternity, independent of creation which was an act of mercy. When God said, "Let us make man in our image," man existed, and the only way God could do it was to become man. So He gave up the memory of his power and wisdom and took on the weakness and limitation of the flesh. In you, *as* you, God is now forming you into his likeness and redeeming everything in your world.

While conscious of being man, you can enter any state and have everything you can imagine. See it. Believe it as yours. Then have faith in the depth of your being. That's all you need to do. But remember, you cannot commit your*self* to that which you do not love. Fall in love with your desire and yield to its fulfillment by becoming it. That is how God became you.

Do not tell another what you want, but "Commune with your own *self* upon your bed and be silent." (Ps 4:4) That *self* is God. Create your desire with your own *self* upon your bed and rest in the knowledge that God will fulfill it for you. As imagination, he is your unseen reality. Seeing only the fruits of imagination, their reality you cannot see, because of God's invisibility.

But one day you will see your invisible self as the Ancient of days. With raiment white as snow and hair like pure wool, he has no beginning and no end. Waiting upon you swiftly and indifferently, regardless of your desire, he kills and makes alive, wounds and heals and none can deliver out of his hands. The world was created by his word, and fulfilled by his power and wisdom to create, called his Son David. When your work is finished, David will awaken you to Fatherhood and change your name to Jesus, the man in whom the will of God is fulfilled. So, man matures when he become his own Father.

The prophet Jeremiah tells us, "The spirit of the Lord will not turn back until it has executed and accomplished the intents of his mind." (Jer 23:20) Your unseen reality will not turn back until you have been transformed into God. As the gods who came down, you assumed the limitation of man to fulfill a predetermined plan and awaken *as* God. Your skull is the holy sepulcher, called Zion. Awakening in that skull, you will come out like a child born of woman. A few months later your power and wisdom, personified as David, is released and your memory restored.

In the meantime, know what you want and construct a scene which would imply you have it. Enter your desire and feel its reality. Then give thanks to the depth of your *self* and fall asleep confident that your unseen reality will execute it for you, and he will.

All things exist right here and now. You can step into any section of time, for a thousand years ago has not passed away, and two thousand years from now is not something to be formed. Everything is! Locked in a section of time, you think it is the only reality, but all things exist *now*. Everything has already been accomplished and is contained, in its completeness, in your skull.

If you want a better job, more money, a nicer car, give it to your *self*. All desires come from the depth of your being. Fulfill them all, for He can see their fulfillment even though you cannot. It costs you nothing to have faith in *self*. Simply assume you are the man you want to be. Yield to that assumption and fall asleep having faith in its unseen reality, for your imagination is God, and without faith it is impossible to please Him.

**"Put on the Lord Jesus Christ and make no provisions for the flesh to gratify its desires."** (Rom 13:14)

"I s not Esau Jacob's brother?" says the Lord. "Yet I have loved Jacob, but I have hated Esau." (Mal 1:2,3) Representing limitation and the body of sense you wear, your brother Esau is hated by the Lord. But if you will fall in love with Jacob and put on the Lord Jesus Christ, all of these limitations will be transcended.

Would you not hate it if you were sentenced to six months in prison, or a lifetime of hard labor? Reason and your senses, representing Esau's world, tell you these are inescapable facts. But Jacob is all imagination. You can fall in love with Jacob by closing your eyes to the prison bars and putting on the Lord Jesus Christ. This is done by assuming you are walking down the main street of town as a free man. Fall in love with this idea and no power on earth can keep it from happening.

Esau, the outer you, came into the world first. His spiritual brother, Jacob, arrived as your breath of life. Jacob is he who wrestles with the Lord. Wrapping the skins of a kid around his hand, Jacob deceived his father into giving him Esau's blessing. His father, thinking he was touching the outer world, felt its reality and gave Jacob's desire the right of birth. Knowing that you always become what you behold, Jacob deceived his father-in-law by stripping the poplar trees and placing the strips before the cattle at the moment of generation. Because of this act, all of the healthy offsprings were born striped and spotted. This deceiving one, in you, is called Jacob in the Old Testament and the Lord Jesus Christ in the New.

In the Book of Isaiah we are told, "For to us a child is born, to us a son is given. The government will be upon his shoulder and his name shall be called 'Wonderful Counselor, Mighty God, Everlasting Father, Prince of Peace.' Of the increase of his government and peace there will be no end." (Isa 9:6,7) These titles will be yours when you practice the law of identical harvest.

Being all spirit, worship God by believing in your spiritual *self*. Wear the Lord Jesus Christ as you would a suit of clothes. Do not accept the evidence of your senses, but believe in your fulfilled desire. Then, when your wish becomes a reality, share your experiences with others and you will be the Wonderful Counselor who is the Holy Spirit.

Ignoring the evidence of your senses and persuading your*self* that you are the man or woman you want to be, you are deceiving your*self*. And, to the degree you are *self*-persuaded, you become. Try believing in your "*self*." Wrestle with the Lord and you will find your assumptions will harden into facts. Then your name will be changed to Israel, for you will be one who rules *as* God. Practicing the good counsel, and putting on the Lord Jesus Christ, you become Mighty God. This title will rapidly be followed by the knowledge of being the Everlasting Father.

When the curtain of God's temple (which is his flesh)

is torn from top to bottom, you will see your *self* as molden gold. Fusing with it, you will ascend into the region of Zion (your skull) and become a member of the order of Melchizedek, for you will be the Prince of Peace forever and ever. Awakening as the Ancient of days you have no father or mother, no beginning of days or end of life. Bearing the four titles of God you will know your*self* to be the Risen Lord.

It is said that when Esau returned and discovered his brother's deception, Jacob disappeared. This is true, for you must close the door of your mind to this sense world (called Esau) in order to open the door and enter the world of imagination (called Jacob). This world vanishes as you make that world alive. Return to this consciousness and Jacob disappears.

The creator of all life is Spirit and must be spiritually worn. As one man, God's heart is as an inflamed ruby where all of the races and nations of the world are contained. You are part of that one man, but pushed out into the world of sense. Learn to fall into and wear your true being, trusting him implicitly. A friend of mine heard the words, "I am just under you, fall to me." She is being urged to make no provisions for her body of flesh and blood, but trust God and fall into a new state of consciousness.

Born into a state of poverty, you may have the desire to transcend these limitations. Man claims you must be educated, meet the right people, or be in the right place at the right time for change to take place. But the Lord says, "I am the way and my ways are past finding out." (Rom 11:33) Try clothing your*self* with the feeling of being what you want to be. Do not be concerned about the scene you create, but what it implies. Eavesdrop on your friends as they hear your good news. Some of them will be happy, while others will show their envy. Let everyone play their part as you listen, all in your imagination. Do you know, you cannot always dictate what they are going to say. You may discover that some are not your friends at all, while others you never knew were so dear, will rejoice. This is the creative power of God, creating through the conscious use of your wonderful human imagination.

As man, you cannot see what God sees, for he goes beyond the facade. He sees and hears what is taking place in the heart. Darkness cannot keep him out, and you cannot hide from him, for he is within you as your I am-ness. All things are possible to him, but you are the operant power. You, and you alone, expand or limit your creativity.

Put on the Lord Jesus Christ and transcend the world of the senses. Consisting of many states of consciousness, you can enter a state knowingly or unknowingly, but all states are permanent. Just as a city does not cease to be because you leave it, poverty remains for anyone to fall into when you depart. Knowing all things exist and are a part of a state of consciousness, know what you want and put yourself in it. Sleep in the state and, if necessary, all of the people who now oppose you, will come to your aid as you move into your desired state.

A prisoner in the world of death, the Lord Jesus Christ comes to set you free. To open your eyes and fulfill your every desire, for he is your own wonderful human imagination. All things are possible to him. If you wear the feeling of success, sleep in it, wake in it and think from its premise, no power on earth can keep you from being successful. If opposition rises, remember, you could not walk if not opposed. The bird could not fly. The fish could not swim. The car could not move, so do not be afraid of opposition.

If you want someone to be important, treat him as though he were. Do it with or without his knowledge or consent. Treat everyone with respect if you want to be respected. Put on your creative power and use your imagination consciously. See the world *as* the Lord Jesus Christ. Know your*self* to be the king of a kingdom that is not of this world. Begin, now, to supplant your brother Esau in the affection of your father. Exercise your divine right and become Jacob, the spiritual man, he who is all imagination.

**"Christ, the power of God and the
wisdom of God."     (1 Cor 1:24)**

I nvisible God, desiring to experience states of
power, extended him*self* by becoming you.
Now housed in a garment called man, invisibility is destined to enter and play the part of the state
called Paul.

Trained in the tradition of his fathers, and knowing
Hebrew backwards and forwards, Paul believed the law
and protected it with his life. But when he discovered
Christ's true identity, he saw the spirit of the law behind
the letter he had protected for so long. Recognizing
Christ to be the power of God and the wisdom of God,
Paul preached only Christ crucified and raised from the
dead. (1 Cor 1:23,24) Seeing the mystery behind the
story he confessed, "Even though I once regarded Christ
from a human point of view, I regard him thus no
longer." (11 Cor. 5:16) Recognizing Jesus Christ as his
own wonderful human imagination, Paul taught that
God's power and wisdom was crucified on and buried in
man, and from man it would be raised.

Only one of the ten commandments the prophet

Moses gave us is positive. It reads, "Honor thy father and mother." (De 5:16) But Jesus tells us, "Anyone who loves father, mother, son or daughter more than me is not worthy of me. For I have not come to abolish the law of the prophets, but to fulfill them." (M't 10:37 & 5:17) Fathers and mothers are the visible cause of the phenomena of life. But you are Jesus Christ, the invisible cause. Learn to love and believe in your*self* more than that which is sense perceived. Love your parents and your children, but do not believe that their lack of money, education or social position is the cause of your experience, for all causation is invisible.

Learn to love this phenomena of life called Jesus. Worship and have no other god besides him. See every experience in life as aspects of your own mind awakening in you. Recognize your father and mother to be the obvious, visible causation, but not the cause of life's phenomena. Its invisible cause is God's creative power, buried in you, as your wonderful I am. This power, called imagination, is God Him*self*.

Paul asks the question, "Do you not realize that Jesus Christ is in you? — unless of course you fail to meet the test." (11 Cor 13:5) Have you tested him lately? A friend of mine did and this is her story. As a free-lance designer she designs primarily for Lanz and Bullocks. Last year Lanz had kept her extremely busy, but when she did not receive a call from them for some time she called to learn that they had employed a full time art director and would no longer need her services. Replacing the phone, she revised the conversation. Hearing them say they liked her work and had lots more for her to do she felt the thrill of the good news. One week later she received a call from Lanz asking her to create a 26-page institutional advertising booklet for them as well as four advertisements for Harper's Magazine. Using her creative power, whenever she needs work she simply imagines being busy, and she is.

Jesus Christ is the creative power of God. By him all things are made, and without him there is not anything made that is made. How are you using God's creative power? Do you believe someone doesn't like you? Is he rude each time you see him? That is Christ in action. You may question why, but you cause him to act the way he does, for there is only one cause and that is Christ. No one can do anything to you unless you have first done it to your*self* by the use of your creative power. Jesus is doing everything and Christ, the power of God in your brain, is what He is doing. "No other foundation can anyone lay than Jesus Christ" (1 Co 3:11) — he who is your own wonderful human imagination.

When truth reveals himself in you, like Paul, you will no longer regard Christ as human, but will see him as your own wonderful human imagination. Exercise this creative power, in you, and watch it grow stronger and stronger through daily use. What must you do to be doing the work of God? Have a desire and imagine it fulfilled. Send forth the feeling of possession and believe in him whom you have sent. Do this and when your desire comes into being you will have discovered the secret of all life.

God, your I am, operates through his creative power which he sent into the world to become you. Christ is not some little man who was born two thousand years ago. His story did not take place never to happen again, but is taking place in the lives of everyone who hears and believes I am He. Believe in your *self* and have faith in your creative power.

Faith is not easy to live by, but do not be like the rebels of Moses. They turned back in search of gods of gold and silver which could be seen. Do not turn back and look for visible causation, because causation is invisible. On this level, the made always reveals the mistakes of the maker, and you learn by your mistakes. Believe in God and his creative power. Learn to live by God's creative power, in you, which is your own wonderful human imagination.

Scripture tells us that Jesus was opposed by Satan. The word means "opponent; the opposite." Everyone has his Satan. If someone tells you something cannot be done, that someone personifies Satan, your doubts or fears. Although things may seem impossible to your reasoning mind, nothing is impossible to imagine, and as you imagine you are using God's power. The world told Edison that indirect current was impossible, but he did not believe it. Instead, he created a machine so perfect that, when tested, nothing needed to be changed. You and I enjoy indirect current today because Edison put Satan behind him.

Christ is the power of God and there is no other power. Nothing or no one can oppose your powerful imagination save Satan, your doubting *self*. If you believe, you can be anything you want to be and have everything you desire to have. Believe in the reality of your imaginal acts and nothing will be impossible to you, for your invisible imagination is the one and only cause of your predominant life.

## A WISE BUILDER

**"No other foundation can anyone lay than that which is laid, which is Jesus Christ." (1 Cor 3:11)**

M an, in his infancy, looks upon everything outside of *self* as the cause of life. But there is only one cause, only one foundation upon which all life is created, and that is your own wonderful human imagination. "You may build on this foundation gold, silver, precious stones, wood, hay or stubble, but your work will become manifest for the day will reveal it." (1 Cor 3:12,13)

Now, if to dream is to dwell in reality, not knowingly for such, what is life for the majority of the world but one long, uninterrupted dream? Calling the dream world shadow and unreal, man gives his dreams interpretations, but how can something unreal be interpreted? Your imagination makes this day and this world alive, just as it does your so-called dreams at night. Consciousness, forever giving reality, causes anything you are no longer aware of to become a memory, just a dream. Therefore, objectivity and subjectivity are wholly determined by where your consciousness is focused. And, since everything contains within it*self* the capacity for symbolic significance, try to interpret your day and night dreams in their symbolic manner, for there is only one foundation. That is your awareness— your imagination.

Imagining all day long, there is never a time when you are not using God's creative power and wisdom. "Let every man take care how he builds upon it. If his work survives he will receive a reward. If it is destroyed he suffers loss but he himself will be saved, but only as through fire." (1 Cor 3:14,15) Be careful what you imagine because, although your imagination is fireproof, the thoughts of the mind will be tested by the fires of experience. If your imagination is conditioned upon someone or something other than *self*, that condition has come between you and Jesus Christ. Such action will cause you to suffer the loss of your desire, but you will be saved, but only as through fire. Believe in your imagination and make it your one solid foundation. All of the "isms" in the world are foundations that are not Jesus Christ, for your imagination is the *only* God. Accept this as your way of life and you will know a freedom you have never known before.

If you want to do the work of God you must feel you are God, for you cannot do the work of one that you are not. If you want your child to live in comfort and freedom, be honored and wanted because of his contribution to the world, tell him he can. If your name is Smith, tell him he is *A* Smith of *THE* Smiths. Make your child feel the importance of your family name, for feeling is the secret of all life. If he accepts what you say, and lives in it, he will become *self*-persuaded. And, because *self*-persuasion is the foundation of all life, he will objectify his belief in *self*.

"You are the temple of the living God and the Spirit of God dwells in you. His temple is holy and that temple you are." (1 Cor 3:16,17) therefore you are already holy. Matthew tells us, "Blessed are the pure in heart for they shall see God." (M't 5:8) Become purified by dying to the delusion that anything outside of *self* can influence your life. Make Christ your only foundation and you will be purified.

A Catholic friend hated the Negro and the Jew. During World War II a Jew saved his life by jumping in front of a hand grenade. Later, while employed as a civilian, his clothes caught fire and a Negro smothered the flames by placing his body on top of my friend. God, in you, knows how to dramatize your delusions. You may think there should be no war, but it comes, and God uses it to die to his delusion concerning a Jew. "All things work together for good to those who love the Lord." (Rom 8:28) A burning body killed his delusion regarding Blacks.

The delusion that Jesus Christ was a child born of a woman called Mary who never knew a man must die. And when it does your mind will release a far greater Jesus Christ than you ever conceived of before. When you see Christ as the cause, the foundation of all life, and firmly believe that you are He, your deep conviction will influence the world.

Forever moving toward the fulfillment of your beliefs, become a wise builder. Take care how you build upon this one foundation, for no other foundation can anyone lay than that which is laid, which is Jesus Christ.

## A LITTLE CHILD

**"Unless you turn and become as a little child
you will never enter the kingdom of heaven."
(M't 18:2)**

A child will believe anything. Tell him a story and, no matter how it is filled with the gossamer of faerie, he will believe it. That is what you are called upon to do. To believe with the simplicity and faith of a little child.

Believe that the body of Jesus Christ transcends all limitations of the flesh, yet is capable of manifesting it*self* within the order of the senses. That it is being woven within you right now. Then use this body by suspending your garment of sense and weaving one of imagination. Paint a beautiful picture of what you would like to be. Move into it. Wear it as you do your garment of flesh and you will be living the imaginative life of a little child.

There are two things which displease the Lord. One is eating of the tree of good and evil (Gen 2:17) and the other is the lack of faith in I am He. (Joh 8:24) Forget all of the so-called good and evil man creates, and fall in love with your desire. Move into the world of imagination and live there, believing in its truth and you will become what you behold.

One beautiful fall day, several years ago, I was tired of making payments on my car, so I imagined its pink slip lying on my dining room table. This would denote, of course, that the car was paid for. Selling real estate at the time, a few weeks later I met a couple who wanted to buy a house. After determining what they wanted, I imagined they had it. During the Christmas holidays my mother called from Kansas to ask if I would visit her the following summer. For one fleeting moment I wondered where I would get the money, but quickly imagined being in her house, then dropped it. A friend called in January to say that they wanted to sell their home. When I showed it to the couple who had expressed a desire for a house last fall, they fell in love with it and purchased it immediately. The commission I received from this transaction paid for my car and my airline tickets to Kansas. There was even money left over to be spent while on the trip. Everything came into being because I imagined and believed as a little child.

"If there is one who judges all men impartially on the record of their deeds and we call him our Father, we should stand in awe of him while we live out the time of our exile." (1 Pet 1:17) Learn to open your spiritual eye while you are exiled, here in the land of death, by seeing the world as one of imagination. Seek the God within *self*, for he is the eternal Father, called Jesus. No one can judge you as harshly, or as impartially, as *self*. Become as a little child and trust this *self*. Believe in him and his power of forgiveness, for he is the Ancient of days, the one David calls Adonai, my Lord.

Belief is essential in all things. Jesus, he who is in you, came and comes to the surface of your being, through belief. Remember the story of Lazarus? Although believing Lazarus to be dead, his sister went to one called Jesus who said, "I am the resurrection and the life, believe in me and all things are resurrected. Do you believe in me?" Then Martha answered, "Yes Lord, I believe you are the Christ, the Son of God who is coming into the world." (Joh 11:25-27) Martha knew Jesus to be the Lord, the Christ, and the Son of God. This knowledge will be yours when God, in you, is raised to a higher level of *self*. This is done by learning to believe as Martha. Can you believe you are the resurrection and the life of all things? That you are Christ, the Messiah, the Son of God who is coming into the world? Start now to believe in your creative power. Exercise your imaginative talent and Christ will rise in you. Then you will no longer see him as a person to be worshipped, but as your own wonderful human imagination.

Intensity is the key. Revelations tells us, "I know your works, you are neither cold nor hot. Would that you were cold or hot. So, because you are lukewarm and neither cold nor hot I will spew you out of my mouth." (Rev 3:15,16) Become as a little child and set your emotions on fire. Add the coals of touch and sound, sight and taste. Intensify your imaginal acts so that their reality is felt and they will be yours. The word "pentacost" means "fire." Pentacost is made alive, in you, when your power manifests itself in the form of wind. Coming out of your brain, the wind will enfold you and awaken you to the knowledge that you are God and everything is possible to your power-filled imagination.

Having told the story of salvation and claiming, "Before Abraham was, I am," Jesus, your awakened body, entered the world *as* you. That which is capable of manifesting him*self* within the order of the flesh, yet transcends all limitations of time and space, used his power to enter the world; thereby vanishing from sight.

*The Invisible You*

Now it is time to turn around. Change your thinking by becoming as a little child and you will enter the kingdom of heaven once more.

## GOD IS LOVE

**"He who does not love does not know God, for God is love."    (1 Joh 4:8)**

God, the author of this fabulous world, is love. Giving him*self* to you in order to experience pain and sorrow, hunger and thirst, heat and cold, He lost all consciousness of his true identity. But the day is coming when his memory will be restored, and on that day you will know that you are love.

It is said that Abraham had two sons, Ishmael and Isaac. Told to take his son Isaac to a mountaintop and offer him as a sacrifice, Abraham built the fire, as requested. As the flames rose Isaac asked, "Where is the lamb for a burnt offering?" and Abraham replied, "God will provide Him*self* the lamb." Although Ishmael was born twelve years before Isaac, the angel of the Lord blessed Abraham for not withholding his *only* son. (Gen 22) This is your story, for in the state of Abraham you became the sacrificial lamb. Consumed, now, in the fires of experience, your son Isaac, the laughing one, the symbol of your resurrection into God, will appear as a sign that you have conquered death and awakened to love once more.

The poet, Hauser, knew this great secret, for it was he who wrote the beautiful hymn, "God Moves in a Mysterious Way His Wonders to Perform." One line of his hymn reads, "Hidden behind this peculiar providence hides a smiling face." This may seem cynical, but it is true. No matter how terrible your world may appear to be, the one who created it is looking into the face of love and smiling, for he is seeing your destiny.

If you were a robot moving through dead space, and God created the universe and gave it to you, would you grow from such a gift? If there were no challenge, no desire, no hunger, no drive, no purpose, and you could not create, would there be any reason for your existence? No. But, because God became the robot, He gave you his wisdom to create and his power to sustain or let go of that which you have created, and God is love. Becoming what He beheld, God beheld you and we are told, "Greater love has no man than this, that man lay down his life for his friends and I have called you friends." (Joh 15:13) Love began a good work in you, and love will finish his work *as* you on the day of Jesus Christ.

One night I fell asleep thinking of the words Christ spoke to his Father when he said, "Return unto me the glory that I had with thee before that the world was." (Joh 17:4,5) That night, in vision, I found my*self* seated behind a desk watching a man pace the floor in front of me. "We have reserved the room and sent out all of the invitations." I said, "Who are we waiting for?" Pointing to a letter on my desk he answered, "The Lord. It is right in front of you." Looking down, I saw a letter I had written but forgotten. Picking it up I read, "I will rejoice in the Lord. His salvation is my resurrection from above."

This is a true vision, for God, having given him*self* to

you, saves him*self* by your resurrection from the dead. His name is I AM. You will resurrect from the skull in which God is buried, for if you did not, God would remain in this world of death forever. You are his salvation, for he died and buried his creative power and wisdom in you that you might live. The day God is saved, the glory you had before that the world was will be restored, and that glory is love.

No one can fail, for "He who began a good work in you will bring it to completion at the day of Jesus Christ." (Phil 1:6) God is the breath of the world. He breathed and your body became a living soul. He did not give you a piece of earth, a star or the universe. No, he gave you a far greater gift than these, for he gave you the gift of *self*. So, set your hope fully upon the grace that is coming to you as God unveils him*self* in you, for God is love.

In the Old Testament we are told, "Our God is a God of salvation and our God is the Lord who escapes from death." (Ps 68:20) How does he do it? By being born anew through the resurrection of Jesus Christ, and unveiling him*self* as love. God gave you his creative power and wisdom. Awaken this power within you and guide all of your thoughts by love. Become conscious of love and you will know who God is. Having no beginning or end, God inserted him*self* into time. When his gift is complete, time will cease to be, for you will become timeless eternity.

*The Invisible You*

**"Be not deceived, God is not mocked, as a man sows, so shall he reap."      (Gal 6:7)**

I n the beginning God gave you a special gift. One that is yours alone. That gift is your mind and speech. With this gift you can create anything and have everything you desire. But, be not deceived, your gift is not mocked, as you sow your thoughts, you reap your world.

The reality of all things is in the human imagination. Its actuality is nothing more than thoughts projected on a screen of space. The room you are now in is real to you, while the adjoining room, regardless of how intimately known, is only a flat surface. Why? Because your God-given imagination gives the room you are now in, reality. Leave it, and it is no longer real, for you are its life. Your friend, like your room, is only a flat surface within you, made alive by the use of your gift of mind and speech.

As all imagination, the immortal you can go anywhere, anytime, do anything and be anyone. Just think you are already there and you will be. If you have received a check for $10,000 what would you do?

Would you just sit and stare at it, or would you jump up and down for joy? Would you bank it, share it or spend it? Do what you would do if the check were yours right now. Use your fabulous gift of mind and speech and tell your friends of your good fortune. Fall asleep investing your heavenly money and, if this principle is true, the money will be yours, for you will have planted a wealthy seed and all things must come forth after their kind. You can change your social or intellectual world the same way, but remember, you cannot deceive your-*self* for your imagination is not mocked. You must persist in the feeling of wealth if you want to enjoy its fruit.

Money is the symbol of security in this world. Thought is your heavenly coin. Invest your heavenly money wisely through the use of audio and video vision. When you think of a friend you can hear his voice as well as see his face. Listen to your friend's good news and believe what you have heard. Feel the thrill of his success and you have planted the seed of fulfillment in your mind. Then one day your friend, he who reflects your thoughts of him, will confirm your vision for all to see.

Discover the secret of imagining, for your world is forever telling you what you are saying to *self*. If told you are not qualified for the new job, or that times are bad, you are reaping doubts you have sown. But, if you really want the job, assume its role. Mentally park your car in your name-space. Sit at your new desk. Read the announcement of your new position in the trade journal. Do everything you would do if the job were yours. Your outer world may show no signs of immediate change, but if you will continue to think *from* your new position (not *of* it) it will be yours. Control your thoughts and, though difficult at first, they will take root and reflect back to you all that has been sown in the mind. Your harvest will come, for you will reap your job, just as you had imagined.

Learn to believe in your true *self*, for all things are possible to him who believes. Have faith in the fulfillment of your desire and, in its own appointed hour, it will ripen and flower. If it seems long in coming, wait, for its harvest is sure and will not be late.

When my first book was just an idea, I applied this principle, and planted the seed of its publication in my mind. I knew no publisher. Did not know how to construct a manuscript, but I did know how to believe in God. As I physically wrote, I mentally saw the book's published form, and rejoiced in its enthusiastic acceptance. The months passed by and, although I could not see any change, I persisted in my assumption.

Then, one day, I was cleaning the hall closet and found a reel of recording tape which had been placed there many years before. Its container bore the name and address of a man I did not know, and a company I had never heard of. Years ago, while Neville was still with us, a man had attended a lecture and given the tape to a friend with the request that the talk be recorded on it. At the time I had a recorder which used a seven-inch reel, as this tape required, and the tape was given to me. But, before transcription was accomplished, my tape recorder was stolen and, as the events of the years passed by, the tape forgotten.

Regretting my thoughtlessness, I quickly placed a note of explanation in the case and returned the tape to its rightful owner, a man who created the best fruitcake in the world called "Grandman's." What a fruitcake! It was truly a "spiritual" feast, filled with bourbon, scotch, gin and just about every "spirit" known to man. I know, for I received one, as well as a letter of thanks for the tape's return. This is how I met the man who told me of the man who published my book. Living in California, I returned a tape to a man in Nebraska who guided me to my publisher in Georgia. And the book? Of course, it's published and enthusiastically received, just as I knew it would be.

This is how God creates, and his spirit dwells in you, just as it does in me. Dare to assume you have what you want. Remain faithful to that assumption and you will have it. But if you do not, it will never be yours. The law is really that simple. Want to live graciously, be a kind, generous person, travel, have a healthy body? Whatever you can think of, you can have, but remember, nothing happens by accident. If you are reaping unhappiness now, you may deny its planting, but God is not mocked. You have to sow unhappy thoughts in order to reap their harvest. Read the morning paper or watch the news on TV and ideas enter your mind. Become discriminating. Carefully select the thoughts you plant, for their harvest will come, and when it does you will not regret the planting.

Believe in your imagination, for it has no handicaps, no bars or limitations other than those you put upon *self*. Believe you cannot be successful because of your social, financial or intellectual background? Then you have placed these conditions upon your imagination. Restrictions, believed to be true, will bar you from success. Limitations denied through lack of consciousness must die, for you are their life. Knowing that all things must bring forth after their kind, become conscious of your gift and plant wisely. But remember, you cannot deceive your*self*, for as you sow, so shall you reap.

## THE SKULL

**"When they came to a place called the skull
there they crucified him."**      **(John 19:17)**

T he events in the life of Jesus Christ cannot
be fixed in time or located in space, for
every time a child is born, he breathes
because Jesus came to a place called the skull and
crucified him*self* there. Loving you, Jesus gave up all
consciousness of being God, to become you. Your skull
is his tomb, and when his dream of life is over, you will
rise from that *self*-same skull to discover that you are
God.

The 42nd Psalm begins, "As the hart longs for flowing
streams, so longs my soul after thee, O God. My soul
thirsts for God, for the living God. These things I
remember—when I went with the throng and led them
in procession to the house of God." (Ps 42:1,2,4) A
moth so hungers for the warmth of the fire that he
voluntarily enters its light and is consumed. Desire with
the intensity of the moth and enter its light. Remain
there until you feel the flame of desire is quenched, and
your desire has been made alive. That is how all things
are made. If your soul longs for an experience of God,

and thirsts for the living God, become consumed with the idea of finding Him and your memory will return. Then you will remember your Good Friday. That day when you led the throng in procession to the house of God where you were crucified. The churches, for reasons of their own, have dated these great events, but they did not and will not take place in time and space, for the death and birth of Christ, in you, are supernatural.

God's dream began in your skull and it is destined to end there. God is dreaming your life into being. Misuse your imagination and you have beaten his divine body, for only imagination can suffer. Cut yourself. Feel pain, and God is suffering, for without awareness there can be no pain. Awareness is imagination, and I am is God's name forever and ever. If asked who was aware of pain would you not say "I am"? John knew this great secret, for his confessions run through his entire book. "I am the door. I am the good shepherd. I am the vine. I am the living water." Your imagination is the great I am recorded there.

Paul tells us, "I have been crucified with Christ; nevertheless I live, yet not I but Christ who lives in me. And the life I now live in the flesh I live by the faith of the Son of God who loved me and gave himself for me." (Gal 2:20) Then he states, "From now on I regard no one from a human point of view, even though I once regarded Christ from the human point of view I regard him thus no longer." (11 Co 5:16) Far from denying Christ, Paul knew the drama was supernatural and that it took place in the skull. It was he who said, "When it pleased God to reveal his Son in me I conferred not with flesh and blood." (Gal 1:16) The churches celebrate scriptural events as having taken place two thousand years ago, but events that take place in the soul cannot be dated. The kingdom of heaven is within you, and you cannot earn it or force its entrance. When the time is fulfilled, your Son will reveal him*self* to you, in the Spirit, and you will know that you are God, the king of kings in your kingdom called heaven.

God, the dreamer in you, has day as well as night dreams. During the night wonderful things are possible. You can be anywhere and in the twinkle of an eye cross a marvelous bridge of events to a completely changed scene. The same is true during the day, when you know who you are. Here's how. Set your*self* a goal and claim you have reached it by viewing the world *from* its premise. Persist, and the dreamer in you will build a bridge of incident which will lead you from where you are now, to the fulfillment of your desire. Then, when it externalizes it*self* (and it will) give credit to the being who gave it to you, for that is how God awakens.

It is said, "As Moses lifted up the serpent in the wilderness, so must the Son of man be lifted up." (Joh 3:14) What did Moses lift up? His creative power. God became the Son of man when his creative power went down into generation and his ideas preceded from there. When, as the Son of man, you lift your power and wisdom by thinking from the premise of being God, you will be as Moses and lift your serpent of generation into regeneration once more.

You are predestined to experience the 42nd Psalm. It is called, "A Maskil of Korah," which means "a special instruction on truth and reality." I invite you to go to the place called the skull and find God there. Awaken him and He will bring all things to your remembrance. Then you will remember when you led the throng in gay procession to the house of God.

## THE "I" OF IMAGINATION

**"I am the living bread that came
down from heaven."    (John 6:41)**

Y our own wonderful human imagination is
personified as Jacob in the Old Testament
and as a man called Jesus Christ in the
New. Imagination is a mighty power which will awaken
in you when you see the world through the "I" (the
awareness of being) God.

Tonight, before you fall asleep, review your day. See
it through the "I" of God. Begin with the day's first
incident and, when you come to a conversation or an
event that displeases you, change it. Hear the words you
want to hear and see the event as you would have desired it to be. Repeat the words over and over again, if
necessary, until you feel that the conversation, or event,
really happened in the flesh. Then continue on until
your day becomes everything you could desire it to be.
If your unpleasant moments are not changed, they will
be repeated, for your "I" has perpetuated them. But
when you have revised and relived your day with the
"I" of God, you have created one which will not recede
into the past, but will advance into the future for you to

experience in its revised form. So do not accept the facts of your day as final—no matter how factual they may be—but repeal them by revising your day, and you will experience a more fulfilling tomorrow.

Awaken the Christ in you by the art of revision, for Jesus Christ is your own wonderful human "I". Turn your attention inward, into the world of thought, and you will discover that everything you formerly believed to exist on the outside, exists only in your imagination. That all of creation is rooted in and ends in your "I".

"I have come down from heaven, not to do my own will but the will of him who sent me, and this is his will, that I should lose nothing of all that he has given me but raise it up at the last day." (Joh 6:38,39) When you descended (in consciousness) you were given every experience in life. Every man, woman or child you meet is a gift from your Father. They are your "I" made visible and come to you because of your attitude towards society or *self*. Regardless of how you feel towards another, you allowed him to descend within you. Your duty is to lift him up within your*self* by revising his words, actions and habits. Then you will discover that he never was the cause of your displeasure, for the cause was within you.

"All that you behold, though it appears without it is within; in your imagination of which this world of mortality is but a shadow." (Wm. Blake) You are the cause of the drama called life. Perhaps you do not like the part you are playing at the present time, but you wrote the script. Having forgotten, you may deny its fatherhood, but the circumstances of your life could not come into being without you. Assert the supremacy of imagination. Do not bow before the dictates of facts, but use your imagination and awaken the "I" of God within you.

When the embodiment of truth, called Jesus, stood

before the embodiment of reason, called Pontius Pilate, reason asked, "What is truth?" and truth remained silent. (John 18:38) Truth sees nothing in pure objectivity, but everything as subjectively related to *self*. You are the source (the cause) of life. If reason, embodied in flesh and blood, stands before you and questions your word, remain silent, knowing that an idea is just a thought to the sleeping man, but a fact to an awakened imagination. Asleep, an idea is just a wish, purely subjective. But when your "I" awakens, all ideas are objectively real. Sleeping imagination is a passive, involuntary acceptance of appearances. But when you voluntarily use your imagination, through revision, you will never again accept anything as true and final unless you desire it that way. You will simply change it, and it will be so. Start now to put your "I" into daily use. Results may come tomorrow, the day after or in a week, but they will come.

In 1905 Albert Einstein startled the scientific world with an equation which is still not fully understood. It was he who said, "Imagination is more important than knowledge. For, if man accepts as final the facts that evidence bears witness to, he will never exercise his God-given means of redemption, which is his imagination."

Open the door of your mind to this wonderful power in you. Revise your day by hearing the man who said, "No, and that's final" say "Yes". Don't discard an unpleasant experience, revise it, for the world is rooted in you. Rivers, mountains, cities, villages, all are human, for they are rooted in your bosom. Therefore, do not let anything fall and remain there. Lift it up, for the will of your Father is this; that of all he has given you, you should lose nothing but raise it up again. It is raised each time you revise your concept of another.

Turn around and see the world subjectively related to

*self.* "Give beauty for ashes, joy for mourning and the spirit of praise for the spirit of heaviness." (Isa 61:3) When a business is failing it has turned to ash. Put beauty in its place by seeing lots of customers and plenty of money coming in. If you are a factory worker, hear the busy hum of machines in full operation. If someone you know mourns, replace it with the sound of joy. Give the spirit of praise for the spirit of heaviness. Lovingly exercise your imagination every day and you will be turned around. Then all of the energies that went down, while you slept, will be turned up once more.

Once the tree of life in the Garden of Eden, you sheltered and fed the nations, comforted the birds and protected the animals from the heat of the day. Cut down by your concept of *self,* you heard a voice from within say, "Do not disturb the roots, for I will water it with the dew of heaven and it will grow again. But this time I will consciously grow to know what and who I am." As the tree of life, you had no conscious knowledge of your majesty. But when your "I" descended into man, you became individualized. One day that "I" which was felled will rise from within *self* to once more become a marvelous tree of righteousness; a planting to the glory of God. That is your destiny.

The true meaning of the word "transfiguration" is "metamorphosis." A complete metamorphosis takes place within you and, just as the grubworm turns into the butterfly, you who believe your*self* to be a man, will know you are God. As a living, animated human being, you will discover that the seeming other is only a branch of *self.* And as you lift the other, your branch comes into leaf as human blossoms appear on your tree of life.

The Son of God sleeps in you. He is the second man, the man of imagination, destined to rule your world. Esau, the man of sense, is only a casing you wear while

Jacob, the inner you, sleeps.

Start now to awaken the "I" of God. Revise your day and project a more beautiful picture on your screen of space. Create a heaven here on earth with your "I" of God—your own wonderful human imagination.

## IMAGINATION IS A PERSON

**"Let us make man in our image." (Gen 1:26)**

God is your deeper *self*, your true being, and God is all imagination. Made in the image of God, you are his personification, his wife 'til the sleep of death is past. As your husband, God is your maker, your slave and redeemer who is forever fulfilling your every thought. Think lovely thoughts and God will fill your life with images of love. Or, if unlovely thoughts are yours, images of hate will appear, for your life is created by your personal thoughts, be they beautiful or ugly.

The surface of your being may be rich or poor, black or white, sick or well. It does not matter who or what you are to God. Radiating through you as the film in your camera is exposed to light, He solidifies as your neighbor, friend or enemy and gives you everything you are imagining. Being a master magician, God wears many forms and faces that you may know what it is like to feel, to touch and to experience. Test this power within you by changing your thinking and watch your magical thoughts change your world.

Let me tell you about my favorite chair. It looked so

sad. The upholstery had worn through in spots, the seat sagged and its color had faded, but I loved it. The upholsterer said it could look like new, but I had no money for his services. So I called upon my deeper *self* and told him of my desire. Loving me as he does, I knew he would never refuse my wishes. So I began to think of my chair as clean, the cushion freshly padded and the upholstery new. Every day I looked at the chair with my imaginary eyes and touched it with my imaginary hands. I made no effort to obtain the money necessary for its repair, but repeatedly thanked my heavenly Father for fulfilling my every desire.

During this time my neighbor's husband became ill and she needed to be with him, as he was in the hospital some 200 miles away. Their son, whom I adore, stayed with us for approximately three weeks while his father recovered. Upon their return I was given a note of gratitude with a $100.00 bill enclosed. This was $20.00 more than the upholsterer wanted, and now my chair is beautiful again, just as I had imagined.

My heavenly Father gave me that which I was conscious of having, and more. Why? Because I persisted in believing in my redeemer. Believing that my imagination would fulfill my every thought. Solidifying as my neighbor, God, the master magician in me, wore her face and furnished the money necessary to fulfill my imagined state. The chair is now upholstered and looks like new again. How long did it take? As long as it took me to change the state from which I was imagining.

The creative power of the universe is pure imagination who speaks to you through desire. Underlining all of your faculties, including perception, this power streams into your surface mind least disguised in the form of productive fancy. You and your thought are one. You are an extension of Jehovah (thought) and are being called back from your *self*-expulsion through infinite levels of awareness. Your dreams, no matter how insignificant, are profoundly important, for in them God speaks to his very *Self*. Look for the symbolism of your dream and, "Learn to live by scripture," (1 Cor 4:6) for your dreams reveal the level on which you stand. They may not follow scripture to the letter, but the eternal message will be there for, although fragmented on the surface of our dream, we are all one at the core. And God is forever calling us back to live in that core as one grand imagination.

Think of your desire as a shadow. Light this shadow with consciousness, and your desire is made real. No one can change unless you, who are in the other, change your thoughts of him. "I am" that which is in the seeming other, for "I" create his shadow. Change your thoughts and you will see him cast his shadow from a more desirable light. The outside world has no power in itself. It is nothing more than the reflection of your imagination. Blake was so right when he said, "All that you behold, though it appears without it is within, in your imagination, of which this world of mortality is but a shadow."

What are the shadows? The house you live in, the clothes you wear, your friends, your job, everything and everyone that enters your world. These are all shadows whose reality is within you. "Man is all imagination and God is man and exists in us and we in him. The eternal body of man is the imagination and that is God him*self*, the divine body Jesus." (Wm. Blake) Return from the surface of your being to your deeper *self* and you will find all men gathered together into one unity which is God. I am cannot go outside of the present time and space for it is the creative power in you. Reflecting a disturbance in you, your world may be turned upside down. But when you change your thoughts, your world will right it*self* again, for everything is taking place in you, the "I" of its beholder.

Know someone who is psychologically disturbed? Don't try to justify the cause, but rearrange the effect. Persuade your*self* that your friend now sees the world in a normal, natural way. Believe he is leading a happy, successful life, and that person will conform to your image. Don't try to treat the shadow from the outside. Start now to treat the person from within, for you are all imagination and imagination is a person called God, the creator of all life.

## THE STORY OF JOB

**"I have heard of thee with the hearing of the ear, but now my eye beholds thee."** (Job 42:5)

T he story of Job is not a study of patience as you have been taught, but one of rebellion. It takes place in the land of Edom where semi-nomads, called Edomites, live. Job is a very rich Arab shiek who has lots of servants, children, sheep, camels, she asses and oxen. As the curtain rises Job, dressed in his finest robes, is standing center stage. One of four woes enters to announce that the Sabeans have slaughtered all of Job's servants and taken his sheep. Then a second woe appears to say that Job's camels are gone and his servants slaughtered. While he is still speaking, a third woe reports the loss of the oxen and she asses. Then a fourth tells of a mighty wind which caused the four corners of the house to collapse killing all of his children. Hearing this Job rents his robe, shaves his head, throws him*self* on the floor and says, "Naked I came from my mother's womb and naked I shall return. Blessed be the name of the Lord." For Job, now being naked, could see nothing to condemn.

Stripped of his children and possessions, the second

act begins as physical destruction, in the form of boils, cover his body from the soles of his feet to the crown of his head. Then Job's wife says, "Are you still going to be honest and your integrity unshaken? Curse God and die." But Job replies, "You have spoken like a foolish woman. Shall God who gave us the good not give us the evil?" Then three friends arrive to comfort him. Believing in retribution—that God will punish the wicked after death or in some future embodiment—they mourn for Job because he must have violated this code in his youth, or in some past lifetime. To them God's justice is even-handed, an eye for an eye, and a tooth for a tooth. But Job feels that is not possible saying, "This judgment far transcends anything I might have done in the past." Then he becomes very *self*-righteous and tells how he has never turned away an infant, fatherless child, widow or stranger. Itemizing all he has done to earn God's grace, the second act comes to its close as Job demands God to appear so that he can present his case face to face.

The curtain rises on the third act as God speaks to Job from out of a whirlwind saying, "Where were you when I created the universe? Who determined its measurements or shut the sea with doors when it burst forth from the womb? Have you commanded the morning or entered into the springs of the sea, the storehouses of snow or hail?" Then Job realizes that no one did anything to him, he did it to him*self* by his own *self*-righteous voice. Repenting, he covers him*self* in ash saying, "I have heard of thee with the hearing of the ear, but now my eye sees thee," for now he sees God as love.

Job had kept every law of the ancient church, sacrificed, followed all of its rituals and yet suffered violently. Then he rebelled and love, commending him for his rebellion, asked him to pray for his friends, and when he did his own captivity was lifted.

That is what you are called upon to do. To forgive yourself by lovingly lifting your friend out of one state of consciousness and placing him in another. This is done mentally, for your friend is not and never has been the state he expresses. He is but the outward picture of the state you have placed him in. Job forgave himself and his friends, by lifting them out of the state of self-righteousness and divine justice and seeing them in the state of grace. Do this, for your world and all of its occupants, is hinged upon your ability to forgive.

In the Book of Luke it is said that when the people told Jesus that Pilot had slaughtered the Galatians and mingled their blood with their sacrifices, Jesus replied, "Do you think that they were worse sinners than those who escaped? I tell you No but unless you repent you will meet a like fate. Do you think that when the tower fell in Jerusalem and crushed eighteen that they were greater offenders than those it did not crush? I tell you, No but unless you repent you shall meet a similar fate." (Lu 13:1-5) When you hear of someone who has been injured or killed and feel that it serves him right, or that it is his just dues, change your thinking or you will meet a like fate. There is no retribution. Every man is simply the personification of a state and is expressing it be it good or evil. You came into this world, not to judge or condemn, but to redeem. Learn to redeem the seeming other, for as you do you save yourself.

If a friend is not well, persuade yourself that he is feeling fine and, to the degree you are self-persuaded, you have lifted him out of the state of illness into the state of health. Don't be concerned as to why he is not feeling well, just change his state and, though his sins are as scarlet they will be as white as snow because of you. Regardless of how many times you fail, keep on trying and then one day God will reveal himself to you and you will say, "I have heard of thee with the hearing of the ear, through the oral traditions of the churches, but now my eye sees thee." And from that day forth you will walk conscious of who you are. You will know that there is no such thing as righteous judgment or divine justice, for when you see love He will embrace you and you and God will be one.

God, like gold in the raw state of ore, became you. He entered the fires of experience for your sake, that you may become pure gold. As the potter, God is not concerned about the garment He wears, anymore than a great sculptor concerns him*self* with the clay he forms. As you, God is expressing every state necessary for you to become his image. And when will that be? On the day of Jesus Christ.

Laying a foundation of infinite states, God created this play of life. Then he put him*self*, as you, through every one of them. Some states cause the occupant to express unlovely thoughts but remember, the occupant is only outpicturing a state. Forgive him by become *self*-persuaded that he is expressing a richer more fulfilling state. Job thought he was being kind and generous when he outwardly clothed and fed the orphan and the widow. Yet, because he did nothing inwardly to change them, they remained as they were. When you see another's need, fulfill it. Do not leave him in the state of desire, but repent and see his desire fulfilled. It is much easier to give a man a dollar than to imagine him gainfully employed, but is it not better to give him the joy of plenty than the embarrassment of lack? You can, for you have a power greater than money. That power is your own wonderful human imagination.

Job, in conflict with him*self*, is the accuser and the accused, for his drama takes place in the mind. The first chapter (inserted by some scribe who could not believe that God would be so cruel) tells of a pact between Satan and God. But the last chapter reads, "They comforted him for all the evil the LORD had brought upon him." (Job 42:11)

Just like Job, you are lost in the confusion of life, thereby causing it to go on and on. But when you realize that there is only one being to whom you can turn, and that being is *self*, perfection comes. Then He who looks like you will appear and you will say, "I have heard of thee with the hearing of the ear, but now my eye beholds thee." For you will know that life, it*self*, is contained *in* you and that all life is an expression of your true *self* who is love.

## THE ROOT AND THE OFFSPRING

**"I am the root and the offspring of David,
the bright morning star."     (Rev. 22:16)**

Although at times you may feel insignificant, you are God, he who created and sustains the universe. As God, the king of kings and lord of Lords, you cut a living portion of your*self* out of the tree of life and implanted it in the physical tree of good and evil you are now wearing. From this tree physical children are born. But when you bear the fruit of the tree of life, God's only Son—he who radiates your glory and bears the express image of your person—will come forth from your spiritual body. And, from that day forward, although your identity of person will remain the same, you will know that you are God, the Father of David.

Searching for his son in the Old Testament God said, "A son is the glory of his father. If I am a father where is my glory?" (Mal 1:6) When your graft is complete your spiritual son will appear and you will understand John's words when he said, "No man has ever seen God but the only begotten Son who is in the bosom of the Father, he has made him known." (Joh 1:18) That is your destiny.

You are destined to bear the fruit of the tree of life, called Christ, and know your*self* to be the root and the offspring of David, the bright morning star.

Have you ever seen a graft performed on a bush or tree? It is a fascinating process. The gardener first finds a healthy branch; one that is capable of propagation. Then it is cut from the parent tree and inserted into a gash made in the stock of another plant. Bound securely, the branch will feed upon the new plant, grow and eventually bear the fruit of its parent, *not* the fruit of the plant to which it is attached.

You are a branch, taken from the tree of life and grafted on the body you wear. Living upon its sap, in time, you will bear the fruit of the tree of life from which you were sent. God, the Father, gave you his name, his awareness, and sent you into the world. And, "As the Father has life in him*self* he has granted (you) his son to have life in your*self*." (Joh 5:26) When your work is finished the identity on which you are grafted will be redeemed.

As the root of all life, as well as its offspring, you are capable of propagation. Belief is your root and that which you believe in is your offspring. Grafting your*self* onto all that you believe to be true, your journey began by believing in a literal, physical world. It will end when your belief is spiritual, for you are a mental traveler, traveling a long, hard road from ritual to *self*-discovery.

If it is your desire to have cities, streets, rivers and mountains named after you, claim their existence in you and it will be so. But if you want that which will never pass away or cease to be, "Set your hope fully upon the grace that is coming to you at the revelation of Jesus Christ in you." (1 Pet 1:13) For when God's Son, the Lord's anointed, stands before you, the revelation of Jesus Christ is yours.

Jesse, the eternal existing one, grafted him*self* on the body you wear in order to experience suffering and hardship, joy and pain. But when your journey is over, God's Son David—he who is the Christ—will reveal your true identity and the spiritual tree of life will bloom in you.

After cutting away a portion of your "I", it was attached to the garment you now wear, thereby giving it life. But when your time is fulfilled a shoot, called David, will spring forth from you and the Spirit of the Lord, in the form of a dove, will descend and remain upon you as a sign that your work is finished. Then the blessings of the Most High are yours.

God came, and comes, into human history in the person of Jesus Christ. You will know that you are he when Christ, the power and wisdom of God, forms him*self* in you and David appears. Then you are transformed. No longer will you think from the premise of being male or female, but from the knowledge that you are God.

"I say, 'You are gods, sons of the Most High, all of you; nevertheless you shall die like men and fall as one man, O ye princes.'" (Ps 82:6,7) Everyone is god, a son of the Most High. Grafted onto humanity all die. But everyone will resurrect the fruit of the tree of life, symbolized as David, and be redeemed, for everyone is God, the root and the offspring of David, the bright morning star.

## BEHOLD THIS DREAMER

**"I have found him of whom Moses in the law and the prophets wrote, Jesus of Nazareth, the son of Joseph."** (John 1:45)

The Book of Genesis begins, "In the beginning God." Then the story is told of one called Joseph who left his home in search of his brothers. When they saw him coming they said to one another, "Behold this dreamer cometh." Joseph was captured and, while a slave in the land of Egypt, he interpreted the dreams of Pharaoh and saved civilization. Then it is said that Joseph died and was placed in a coffin in Egypt.

You are that dreamer, called Joseph, and the body of flesh you now wear is your coffin. As God, you had to leave your heavenly home in order to experience individual life. Now asleep to your true identity, you are the immortal dreamer whose dreams can save the world. Joseph saved civilization from starvation by understanding the universal language of symbolism and making earthly preparations based upon his dreams. Rising to the height of *self*, he forgave his brothers and was given the power of Pharaoh. This is your destiny.

Behold this dreamer who creates your life through the power to see, touch, hear, taste and smell that which is not physically present. These invisible organs, asleep, are Joseph, for they are unaware of what they are doing. Awaken Joseph by commanding each organ to do your conscious will. Test your power to hear that which is not physically present, to see what your physical eye cannot see, to taste, touch and smell anything you can conceive. Your physical mother need not be present to feel her presence or hear her voice. You can see as well as smell money even though none is present, for Christ (your creative power) does not need physical evidence to believe things into being. He simply dreams and the world responds.

We are told that just before God fell asleep he said to Moses, "The time has come for you to sleep with your fathers; then this people will rise and play the part of the harlot with strange gods of the land where they go to make them alive. And I will hide my face from them on account of all the evil they have done because they have turned and worshipped other gods." (Deut 31:16,18) Here we see that idolatry is equated with the harlot. Asleep you believe God is external to *self* and play the part of the harlot by believing there is life outside of *self*. But there is only one God. He is your maker and your husband. His name is I AM. It is He who touched your mother and heard her voice. It was God who saw the money and smelled its pungent odor, for you cannot touch, taste, hear, see or smell anything without being aware of it, and awareness is saying I AM.

Awake O sleeper from the land of dreams and return to the only true God who is within you. You were God in the beginning. Then you left your home in the state of Abraham and buried your *self* in your physical body, which you must wear while you pass through the states of Isaac and Jacob. Then your journey will come to its end in the state called Jesus Christ, for it is there that you awaken as God Him*self*, the creator of it all.

Joseph, the husband of Mary in the New Testament, is the same Joseph as is recorded in the Old Testament. Awakening to his true identity in the New, his name is changed from Joseph to Jesus. Read your New Testament carefully and you will note that after Jesus was twelve years old (the age of puberty) Joseph is spoken of no more, but "Jesus increased in wisdom and in stature and in favor with God and man." (Lu 2:52)

Behold this dreamer, Joseph, sleeps in you, but when he awakes you are Jesus Christ, the hope of glory. The divine body, in you, and the creator of all life, is Christ. He can perform any magical act you can conceive, for all things are possible to him. Test him. If you are financially embarrassed, allow him to fill your house with gold. Become a Midas and watch everything you touch turn to gold. Light your consciousness with the feeling of wealth and all things related to the state will flow into your life. You have the power to feel a fifty dollar gold piece, see a loved one or hear the jealous voice of a friend. Awaken this inner you, for he is the eternal vine from which all things grow. Learn to trust him, for nothing is impossible to God who is dreaming he is you.

Start now to bring your imaginary senses into play, for everything in life must be first imagined. The greatest painting had its creation in the artist's imagination. Its beauty is recorded on canvas, but its reality is in the mind. Make daring experiments with Christ. Become familiar with him, for through him all things are made and without him is not anything made that is made. Then one day you will find him of whom Moses in the law and the prophets wrote, Jesus of Nazareth, the son of Joseph. And when you do it will be the Invisible You!

## IMITATE GOD

**"Be imitators of God as dear
children."**     (Eph. 5:1)

G od created this world with a wish saying,
"Let us make man in our image." He persisted and His wish came true. Imitate God
by living as one possessed by a wish and your wish will
become your reality.

When my son was very young I gave him the Sears
Christmas catalog and told him that this was his "wish"
book. From it he could choose what he wanted Santa to
bring him for Christmas. From the day the book
arrived, until the day of Santa's visit, his "wish" book
was by his side. Every year, for eight years, the same
drama was played out in our house. But on the eighth
year the catalog arrived with a new title. That year, and
for many years thereafter, the catalog was called, the
"Sears *Wish* Book." Whoever had that account thought
they had created an original idea, but I had created it
eight years before, for there is no fiction. How can there
be fiction when imagining creates reality?

Why not play the game of wishing by thinking of life
as God's "wish" book. A book filled with every desire of

your heart. A book where you can pick and choose what you want God to give you, then accept his gift by claiming it is yours. If you would but lose your*self* in the feeling of possession, God, plus time, will give it to you in this world of space.

A friend of mine looked into God's Wish Book and found the condominium of her dreams. Everything she had ever desired in a home was to be found there. Owning a house with her sister, and both desiring to sell, they put the house on the market while she placed a deposit on her dreamed-of condominium. Three months passed. The house did not sell and the deposit, as well as the new apartment, was lost. Everything on the outside said the condominium could never be hers. But she moved into her wish by sleeping there every night in her imagination. Carrying groceries down its long hall she cooked in its kitchen. Night after night she fell asleep saying, "I can't lose anything, and now live in this wonderful home." Four months later the house was sold. Returning to the condominium office, with money in hand, my friend learned that the apartment had been sold, twice, for $5,000 more than she had agreed to pay for it. But, since the new owners were unable to raise the money required, the apartment was available. My friend bought her dream condominium, at her original price, with her original down payment as a deposit. She is living there now and told me, "I think the apartment kept improving the four months I was sleeping in it, for it is so much better than I remembered."

Jeremiah tells us, "The will of the Lord will not turn back until he has executed and accomplished the intents of his mind." (Jer 23:20) His will is to fulfill your every thought. As the Lord, the creator of all life, my friend clothed her*self* in her desire. She wrapped the consciousness of its fulfillment about her as you would a suit of clothes. Although the feeling was sometimes difficult to maintain, she would not allow her thoughts to turn back to reason and doubt, but walked in the awareness of her new home by day and slept in it at night. Her will would not turn back until she had executed and accomplished the intents of her mind, and her thoughts became her reality.

Jesus Christ is the fulfillment of God's wish. You are the word that went forth from God's mouth which cannot return unto him void, but must accomplish that which was purposed and prosper in the thing for which you were sent. Your heavenly Father will reveal this truth, in you, for you are predestined to become your own image. To reflect God's glory and bear the express image of his person.

When asked, "Who do men say that the Son of man is?" those in attendance replied, "Some say John the Baptist, others Elijah, Jeremiah or one of the prophets." But when asked, "Who do you say that I am?" Peter answered, "You are the Christ, the Son of the living God." (M't 16) Think of another as God's Son and you have given your kingship away. But when his word is made alive, in you, you will know you are the Christ, the Son of the Risen Lord.

The Bible, in its manuscript form, was given to the evangelists in paragraphs, each complete within itself and independent of each other. Although many tried to compile God's story, we have only four books, namely: Matthew, Mark, Luke and John. Luke did not claim his chronological presentation to be more exact than the others, but felt he had made better use of the source material saying, "Inasmuch as many have undertaken to compile a narrative of the things that have been happening among us by those who were eye witnesses from the very beginning as ministers of the word, it seemed good to me also to write an orderly account that you may know the truth." (Lu 1:1-4) John does not mention the birth or its symbolism, but states simply that you must be born from above. But, because of Luke, the world believes Christ, whose Father is God and Spirit, was born through the womb of a woman, and it isn't so at all. God possessed you, and possessing you He became you. Fall in love with the true story of salvation, for God's gift of grace was bestowed upon you before that the world was, and you *must* fulfill His word. Regardless of your social, financial, or intellectual background remember, the least in the kingdom is greater than the greatest man on earth.

But, while you are here, exercise your imagination. Become imitators of God as dear children. Make a composite picture of what you want. Enter it and lose your*self* in the feeling of fulfillment. With belief as your camera and faith as its film, snap the shutter and your picture is ready for development. As time goes by conflicting circumstances may appear, but do not be dismayed, for conflict may be essential to your desires' fulfillment. Just wait. Your picture will be developed on time, and you will see its image in living color on your screen of space.

Live each day as one possessed by a dream. Feel you now have that which you formerly desired. It is never too late. The world and all within it is your wish book. Start now to imitate God. Live as one possessed by a dream and your dream will become your reality.

## THE COIN OF HEAVEN

**"The word is very near you; it is in your mouth and in your heart so that you can do it."   (Deut 30:14)**

A coin, be it earthly or heavenly, has two sides. The earthly coin is visible and used to purchase things of this world, while the heavenly coin is invisible, yet without it your world would cease to be. In a work called the *Hermetica*, which came out in the first century and translated into four volumes by Walter Scott, it is said, "There are two gifts which God gave to man alone and to no other mortal creatures. These gifts are mind and speech which are equivalent to immortality. If a man uses these gifts aright, he will differ in nothing from the immortals. And when he sheds his body they will be his guides. By them he will be taken into the troop of the gods and into the souls of those who have attained to bliss." This is God's gift to you, for your two-sided coin of heaven is your mind and speech.

Possessing the power to form thoughts into words, you can take your invisible thoughts and form them into words that would imply the fulfillment of every desire of your heart. If you will but "Say to this mountain, 'Be taken up and cast into the sea' and you do not doubt in your heart, but believe that what you say will come to pass, it will be done for you." (Mark 11:23) The mountain may be an enormous problem, or a visible opposition to your goal, but if you will say to it, "Be removed and cast into the sea" and will not doubt in your heart, it will be done for you. So pray, by using your heavenly coin, and believe your prayer has been answered and it will. Do not be concerned as to the how, when or where it is going to appear. Only believe that your heavenly coin will never return unto you void, but must accomplish that which you purposed and prosper in the thing for which it was spent.

Since speech is the image of the mind, we are urged to "Put off your old nature which belongs to your former conversations, and put on the new nature created after the likeness of God." (Eph 4:22-24) In other words, change your old habitual thoughts and construct new ones after the likeness of your desire. Then listen to your inner speech, for it is the image of God called "The word which is very near you; it is in your mouth and in your heart so that you can do it. 'See, I have set before you this day good and evil, life and death, blessing and curse; therefore choose life that you and your descendants may live." (Deut 30:14,15,19) You have the right of choice, but are urged to choose life that you may live more abundantly. Having the ability to speak and form thoughts, as well as the choice of life or death, good or evil, blessing or curse, I hope you choose life, good and blessings, but the choice is up to you.

Every moment of time you are thinking, carrying on inner conversations, treading the winepress and making your wine bitter or sweet. When you hear a friend tell you his good news and feel the joy of the hearing, sweet wine is yours. But if you remember a cruel remark you drink the bitter wine of its sting. God never waivered from his promise to make man in his image. Imitate God by using your heavenly coin to make your wishes in your image. In the Book of Psalms it is said, "To him who orders his conversations aright I will show the salvation of God." (Ps 50:23) If you will but order your conversations aright, by forming your desired thoughts into words, you will see the salvation of imagination, for you will save your*self* from missing your desires.

Since life is given through feeling, "Be angry but sin not." (Ps 4:4) In other words, blow your top if you must, but revise the experience. Change the hour or the day so that joy is felt rather than anger, and you have not sinned, for to sin is to feel that your desire is unfulfilled. But if you feel that your wish is fulfilled you are investing your coin of heaven wisely. Then you will differ in no respect from the immortals (those who have complete control of their thoughts and inner speech) and when you shed your body they will be your guides into the troop of the gods and into the souls of those who have attained to bliss.

Since God became you every word you hear is His. He creates your world by the use of your heavenly coin. Use it wisely. No one can stop you from being what you want to be but your invisible *self*. Invest your coin of heaven by giving thanks to God for his invisible gift, and bless the world you are.